# Options from Within

## Learning to Love Yourself and be Loved.

A series of vignettes designed to help
repair, restore and reinforce
your self-esteem!

Jacques Weisel

**KENDALL/HUNT PUBLISHING COMPANY**
2460 Kerper Boulevard   P.O. Box 539   Dubuque, Iowa 52004-0539

Text and Cover design by GRAPHLINK™
David R. Leaman, C.D.

ISBN 0-8403-8096-8

Printed in the United States of America.
10  9  8  7  6  5  4  3  2  1

# Dedication

This book is lovingly dedicated to all the men and women who are seeking *peace of mind* through Personal Growth!

# Acknowledgements

Dr. Wayne Dyer...who first suggested I write the book.

Leo Buscaglia...the love guru.

Janine Burns, Reverend...for spiritual motivation.

David Leaman...for the great artwork involved.

Ann Lorenz...whose nimble fingers put it all together.

Janet and Joseph...wife and son, my ultimate motivators.

# What World Class Motivational Authors
## Say About
### JACQUES WEISEL

"This wonderful book will inform, inspire and elevate you to higher levels of self esteem and personal awareness. Jacques Weisel has written a guide book to the human spirit that provides you with insights and ideas to guide you more smoothly over the bumpy road of life. Jacques, I hope you sell a million copies and become a nationally renowned author."

**BRIAN TRACY**
**...author of THE PSYCHOLOGY OF**
**ACHIEVEMENT and SUCCESS SECRETS**
**OF SELF-MADE MILLIONAIRES.**

"Your outline is great, your material is superb, your credentials are outstanding."

**WAYNE DYER**
**...author of YOU'LL SEE IT**
**WHEN YOU BELIEVE IT!**

"The world desperately needs the inspired, insightful and totally helpful thinking of Jacques Weisel. Jacques truly utilizes his Options From Within and can captivate and motivate you to do as much or more than he has done, and his accomplishments are great". Jacques writes in brilliantly self illuminating thought bullets—that taste good, refresh one's spirit and make one's life take on new meaning and purpose. I love his thoughtful insights that make me smile, laugh, think and grow wiser."

**MARK VICTOR HANSEN**
**...author of HOW TO ACHIEVE TOTAL**
**PROSPERITY and DARE TO WIN.**

"Congratulations on your obvious commitment to excellence and to sharing empowering insights with others. This book was clearly a labor of love for you!"

**ANTHONY ROBBINS**
**...author of UNLIMITED POWER.**

# Contents

# Introduction

This book actually began to write itself in 1981, as a series of articles written for the GRAPHIC, a local paper on the South Shore of Long Island, New York. As the years progressed, I continued to write many articles, most of which were published in national business magazines. Add to this the letters to newspaper editors, T.V. scripts et. al., and you have a plethora of material from which to choose.

For these reasons I recommend you treat this book like a "life buffet"; taste it all, then go back for what you like, and have a feast.

As you treat your mental taste-buds to the material herewith presented, you'll find your curiosity renewed, and you'll return to the banquet-table again and again.

To keep it moving, I've inserted new and original vignettes of life between the original columns, thus insuring the up-to-datedness of my contribution to the literary world.

In June 1984, I submitted the 43 columns...titled "Positive Living" to the New York-INTERNATIONAL ASSOCIATION OF BUSINESS COMMUNI-CATORS' 50TH Anniversary Literary Contest. I received the Bronze Award for "a series of articles". This encouraged me to send them to a new, up-and-coming magazine entitled PERSONAL SELLING POWER. They trimmed down and published 10 articles, once again under the Positive Living pennant. The articles then found their way to other magazines, notably THE HOT BUTTONEER...a publication for Sales & Sales Management Training. Although most of my material until then had to do with Attitude rather than Aptitude, it seemed the times were ripe for less training and more motivation in the workplace. Current research proves this to be true today as well. People want less How-Tos and more Help Me To Want Tos.

As a direct result of reading my columns in Personal Selling Power, *Dr. Wayne Dyer* wrote several times to me, suggesting I write a book based on the columns. To quote Dr. Dyer: "Your outline is great, your material superb, and your credentials outstanding!...don't write it because you want a book published, write it from your "kishkas" (Yiddish for "guts") because you have to say it. Write for You, Not Them. The publication will become a bonus-" (end of quote)

So here I am, seven years later...spilling my guts! Hope you learn from reading this as much as I learned writing it!

# WHAT'S HOLDING YOU BACK?

Right now I'm going to help you discover the single biggest obstacle to your success in life. It's important, so stay with me. OK?

Now, answer this question:

What's holding you back?

I mean what's really holding you back?

What's preventing you from enjoying life to its fullest? From being that happy, healthy, financially secure adult you dreamed about being when you were a child?

Is it your environment? Your spouse? Your parents? Your boss? Is it your lack of education or a lack of money? Were you born under the wrong stars? Or have you experienced a lot of plain, old-fashioned bad luck?

Whatever it is, write it down. Right now. On a piece of paper. On any piece of paper that's close at hand--even a napkin or the back of an envelope.

Ready? Okay. Now, I'm going to call your bluff. There are two things I know about you already. First, you didn't write anything down. You only thought about what you should have put in writing.

Putting your thoughts and plans in writing has been proven time and again to be one of the most important steps you can take to help your dreams become reality. Yet, only 4 to 5 percent of adults actually use this simple success strategy!

Second, the reasons you give for not accomplishing more with your life are nothing but excuses. I know they don't seem like excuses to you. But that's because you are reacting to the situations you find yourself in--not acting on them. You have gotten into the habit of thinking nothing you do can change your life much.

No one leads a trouble-free life. All of us are oppressed and suppressed in one way or another by our environment, our families, and the society in which we live. Yet, few of the people who are truly successful in life have any more intelligence, innate ability, or luck than you have now.

The biggest difference between people who lead fulfilling lives and those who just get by is simply this:

*Successful people believe in themselves.*

They believe they can reach whatever goal they set out to reach, and they pursue those goals, *despite all obstacles*, until they make their beliefs turn into reality.

Thomas Edison failed thousands of times before he invented a light bulb that worked. Yet, he kept on trying. Because of his belief and persistence, candles have become decorative home accessories--instead of everyday necessities.

If you believe in yourself, if you believe you really deserve to share in life's riches and if you persist relentlessly in your quest for those riches, you will find a way to overcome each obstacle that gets in your way.

But, if deep down in your heart you don't believe you're mentally or spiritually good enough to succeed, you will find a thousand reasons to continue to fail. And you will use those reasons to isolate yourself from the very things in life you most want to possess.

Is that just a lot of hogwash dreamed up by Twentieth Century psychologists? Not at all. It is the underlying principle of success that has been observed and passed down by great thinkers and philosophers throughout the history of mankind. King Solomon put it this way:

*As man thinketh in his heart, so he is.*

In 500 B.C. Buddha proclaimed:

*All that we are is the result of what we have thought.*

And, Roman Emperor Marcus Aurelius said:

*A man's life is what his thoughts make of it.*

Unfortunately, most people believe they can't do anything about the circumstances in which they find themselves. So they stop trying. They are never really happy, never really financially successful, because they don't believe in their innate ability to achieve what they desire in life.

As a result, they become victims of the "I can't...because..." syndrome. They retreat mentally, and, sometimes physically, from the life they would like to lead because they don't believe it can ever be theirs.

Now I ask you, aren't you tired of saying, "I can't...because?"

Aren't you tired of giving yourself all the same old excuses for not succeeding? Aren't you sick of hearing yourself say:

"I don't have enough time."

"I don't have enough money."

"I don't have enough education."

"I'm not smart enough."

"My wife doesn't back me up."

"My husband abuses me."

"My parents don't love me."

"My boss doesn't like me."

"Nobody listens to me."

"I can't do anything right."

Etcetera, Etcetera, Etcetera...!

There are an endless number of excuses you can--and do--use for continuing to fail--for not doing what you really want to do--for not acquiring what you wish and dream could be yours.

But you don't have to settle for a life full of excuses. You can take

3

control of your life and turn it around!

## What Excuses Really Mean

If you examine each of you "favorite" excuses closely, if you really think carefully about what it is you are saying each time you give yourself another excuse, you'll realize all of your excuses could be expressed in the same three words: "I'm no good!" I'm not good enough for my parents to love me. I'm not good enough to keep my husband from abusing me; I'm not good enough to get a job done the right way, ....

Truth in a Crudity

How common is that sentiment? How many people feel deep down inside of themselves that they are "no good"?

Behavioral psychologists put the figure at close to 80 percent of the population. Surprisingly, many people who appear to be leading successful lives, who seem to have everything they want in life, actually view themselves as failures because of one imagined personal shortcoming or another.

On four separate occasions recently, I have had individuals who appear to be highly successful tell me how utterly worthless they felt. One is the owner of two thriving businesses; another is a public speaker who, a number of times, had spoken from the same podium with such notables as Dr. Norman Vincent Peale and (at the time) Governor Ronald Reagan; the third is the owner of a successful job placement service; and the fourth is a nutrition/human potential lecturer.

To my surprise, each of these people (who do not know one another) expressed the same sentiment about themselves. And each expressed that sentiment using the same blunt and rather crude phrase:

*"Sometimes I feel like I'm nothing but a piece of shit!"*

How many times have you said or thought those words? How many times have you accused the people around you of making you feel that way? More importantly, why did you describe yourself in terms of something so worthless and repulsive? Something not even good enough to walk on?

The answer is that you—along with over 80 percent of the people with whom you come in contact every day—have little or no self-esteem.

## How Negatives Get Programmed Into Our Thinking

Why is it that most people fail to develop a healthy self-esteem? Virtually all of our lives we are surrounded by negativity. Before we reach the age of five, we are programmed with 15,000 negative words and phrases. The words "no", "can't", "don't", "bad", "be quiet" and many other negatives are repeated to us over and over and over again.

Frequently those words are followed by these admonitions: "You'll get hurt." "You'll get sick." "You'll be punished." "You'll make a mess." "You'll ruin it." "The policeman will take you away." "I won't love you anymore."

When we are children, our natural curiosity and excitement are viewed

4

with suspicion, rigidity, fear (that we'll get hurt), and even anger. Small wonder we learn to suppress our positive strivings.

When the time for school comes, we are greeted with an emphasis on conformity rather than creativity. In an attempt to fit in and get along in our new world of the classroom, we drop the positive need to go our own way--and who would blame us?

If we don't stop talking when the teacher says to be quiet, if we don't sit down when the teacher says to sit down, if we dare to ask questions about something the teacher doesn't want to discuss at the time, if we don't memorize the answers the teacher wants us to, we are scolded or punished. And if we don't act the way the other children act, wear the same kind of clothes, play the same games, laugh at the same jokes, they laugh at us, ostracize and reject us.

We are bombarded by advertisements that make us feel self-conscious, unattractive, unhealthy, uncaring or dissatisfied with our possessions. Think how many times you have been told by one ad or another that you have bad breath, obnoxious body odors, discolored teeth or dentures. That you are unattractive because you don't wear the right clothes, you are too fat, too skinny, have frizzy hair, too little hair--or hair in the wrong places. That your house is an unpleasant or unhealthy place to live because your carpets don't smell fresh, or you haven't eliminated all the germs from the kitchen, bathroom, or--heaven forbid--the baby's room. That your child isn't doing better in reading or math, or is going to have trouble passing the college entrance exams because you haven't bought him or her a computer.

The programs we watch on television aren't any better. Do they teach us to respect ourselves and others? Do they teach us to enjoy life?

Not at all. They portray life as a commodity that is cheap, meaningless, dispensable and fraught with problems. Sponsors of TV programs seem to be more interested in showing us what they think we would like to see, rather than what we should see. And there hangs the awful truth. For the more sex and violence we see, the more we take it for granted and the more we want to see.

The American Council of Life Insurance tells us that a child growing up today will have witnessed over 18,000 murders on TV (and, incidentally, watches more than 35,000 commercials) by the time he or she is ready to graduate from high school. Think how many murders (and commercials) you have watched if you're 40 years old!

If you're a fan of soap operas or of that white-haired guru of problems--Phil Donahue--think how many times you've wallowed in the sorrows--both real and imagined--of other people. There is nothing therapeutic in reliving your problems by hearing others repeat them or act them out before millions of viewers.

How can you really believe you can accomplish anything significant in life when you keep hearing people say how bad life has been to them? When you commiserate with their problems time and time again? After all, how many people call in or appear on shows like the Donahue show to talk

5

about how happy they are?

What about the newspapers? Do the articles we read provide us with a more positive view of life?

Out of curiosity one day, I picked up the two largest selling newspapers on Long Island and tried to determine how much good news appeared in the papers. The results were predictable. My analysis showed that 87% of the news was bad.

Funny thing about statistics. William James of Harvard, who is known as the father of modern psychology, tells us the average person only uses 5 to 10 percent of his full potential. He also reads newspapers where only about 5 to 10 percent of the news is good. Is this a coincidence? Or are we smart enough to see the direct connection between what we feed into our minds and what will come out?

To rephrase Marcus Aurelius:

*We become what we think about all day long.*

When we listen to the problems of others, when we read about them in print, when we see them acted out on TV shows or in the movies, we are continually programming problems into our own lives.

Need a little proof? According to Norman Cousins, fully one-third of medical students take on the symptoms of the disease they are currently studying.

On the flip side of the coin, scientific studies published in the book, *Placebo Theory, Research and Mechanics* show placebos have been proven to release substances within the brain which act as pain killers and which can activate the body's immunological system.

Add the greatest of all negative catchalls, guilt, to the other destructive influences in an individual's life and you will have described the average neurotic, low self-esteemed American. He or she has been chastised as a child for upsetting Mama, and, as an adult, for not living up to Dad's expectations. He has learned, like Pavlov's dog to respond at the sound of the negative bell, and to drink from the saucer of disillusionment.

### What We Should Have Been Taught

Instead of being told what we could not, should not, or dare not do, we should have been reminded of our uniqueness as individuals. We should have been told of the *spark of divinity* instilled in each of us at birth. Science recognizes only two infinites—outer space and inner space—the human mind.

The mind is a three pound mass of cells that can store up to one hundred *trillion* bits of information. When necessary, it can handle over 6 trillion chemical reactions and up to fifteen thousand decisions *per second*, as in the case of the digestive process following eating. Our sense of touch can detect a projection only one twenty-five thousandth of an inch high. We can taste one part quinine in two million parts water. We can smell up to ten thousand different odors. Our body produces every chemical needed to heal itself. Each of us is literally a mass of positive potential.

Moreover, every one of us is capable of accomplishing anything that has ever been done by anyone in the world to date--if we will but develop a healthy self-esteem.

Nobel Prize winner John Steinbeck wrote:

"It is the nature of man to rise to greatness, if greatness is expected of him."

Remember those words, because you can rise to greatness if you expect greatness of yourself.

GIGO

Computer programmers have a term to describe what happens when you feed information into a computer--GIGO. It's an acronym for

Garbage In; Garbage Out

Tell me, what are you feeding your mind? True, as a child you were at the mercy of parents, teachers and other adults who fed you their brand of propaganda. What now? Do you have the guts to take stock of your personal life? Can you decide what's wrong with it, and change it?

No matter what your past experiences have been, you can improve your life.

No matter how long you have been living in a world infested by negativity, you can start living positively.

No matter how many excuses you have given yourself in the past, and how rotten, how *really rotten* you feel about yourself right now, you can turn your life around. And you can start right this minute! Positive Living is not a Utopian dream or an unreachable star. It can be your reality--if you choose to let it be.

Of course you could keep giving yourself alibis and excuses for not living the life you would like to live. In fact you could probably invent a thousand reasons for continuing to *fail.*

But all you really need to take full control of your life--to turn your life completely around is one good reason. What is that reason?

I'm worthy!

*I'm Worthy!*

Did you say those words out loud and with a lot of emphasis and conviction? Or did you mutter them under your breath--so no one could hear?

I thought so. Now say them out loud. If you feel self-conscious, go someplace where no one can hear you (the basement, the backyard, the bathroom). But say them out loud. Say them with conviction. Remember:

*You will become what you think about all day long.*

Change or Stay the Same--the Ultimate Choice is Yours!

Psychologists tell us we only change our attitudinal traits on an average of 2% a year. That means unless you make a conscious effort to change your way of thinking you can expect to become a new and improved (I stole that from the ads) person every 50 years or so.

Do you really want to wait that long? No?

I didn't think so. If you're not happy with yourself right now, you can accelerate your personal growth pattern very easily. How? By replacing your old, tiresome, negative thoughts with stronger, positive ones. Daily application of the positive living techniques in this book can change lives and personal fortunes.

How long will it take? Making your dreams come true will hopefully take you a whole lifetime. As you begin to live one dream, reach one plateau in your life, you will start to formulate new dreams and hopes to achieve. The important thing is you can make that first and most important step *right now*.

Psychologists tell us it takes as little as 21 days of concerted effort to break a habit. Negative thinking is simply a bad habit that you have absorbed like a sponge from the world around you. Just as you can use the power in your hands to get rid of the water in a sponge, you can use the power in your mind to get rid of the habit of negative thinking. All you have to do is try hard enough.

Now I ask you this. How was your day today? How was it *really?* Didn't like it much? Remember that the power to change is in you. Don't let things happen to you. Make things happen--your way! First, believe in your mind it can be done--and then do it! Start right now, and you will begin to build a better life in as few as 21 days.

### How Do You Get Started?

You can sit around all day thinking positive thoughts and nothing is going to happen. You have to *act* on your positive thoughts to make a difference.

Now here's the first action I want you to take.

At the beginning of this chapter I asked you to make a list of all the things that are holding you back from leading a happier, healthier life. Well, if you didn't make that list, go make it now.

Get a big sheet of paper and write down everything you can think of that stands in the way of your success. Go back and look at the list of excuses in the middle of the chapter. Be sure your list includes all of your "favorites", including any not printed in the book.

When you're finished, tear the paper in half. Now tear the two pieces in half. Keep tearing up the paper until you have a mound of little scraps you can't tear any more. Now, if you have a fireplace or other safe place, burn the scraps of paper. If you can't burn them, scoop them all into the garbage.

Why am I asking you to do such a ridiculous thing? Just as you have the power to shred up your list of excuses, you have the power to remove the obstacles to your success. You just have to keep working at it until those obstacles become no more significant than the ashes in the fireplace or the scraps of paper in the garbage pail.

Don't worry if you feel silly doing it. Or if it seems meaningless to you. *Do it.* The action will reinforce what you've been reading and help imprint a new positive attitude in your mind.

## Start Building Your Self-Esteem

Here's another thing I want you to do right now. Copy the sentence below on two sheets of paper. Put one in your house and one in your wallet. Then every day this week take a minute in the morning, at lunch time and in the evening to reread the message you've written. Like ripping up your list of obstacles rereading the message frequently will help imprint it on your mind.

Here's what you should write and read every day:

*Whatever my mind can conceive and believe, I can achieve.*

And, here's the last thing I want you to do this week. First, praise yourself for something every morning and every night. If you've done something terrific--like clinching a new account--tell yourself so--just as you might praise yourself for dong something ordinary. Did you get out of the house on time? Remember to turn off the bathroom light so you'll save a few pennies? Did you wait a second when the traffic light turned green so the car on the other side of the road could make his left turn across traffic?

Most of life is made up of ordinary experiences, and, if we are proud of the ordinary things we do, we have a lot to be proud of.

Remember you were born alone, and will die alone. Change must also come on an *individual* basis. Accept your unique qualities, your God-given divinity. And keep in mind what Goethe said more than a century and a half ago:

*"What you are is God's gift to you.*

*What you make of yourself is your gift to God."*

The title of this first chapter reads: WHAT'S HOLDING YOU BACK? I believe you are now ready to change it once and for all to what it really is: WHO'S HOLDING YOU BACK? I also believe you are ready to handle the fact that YOU are the only obstacle you need to overcome in order to make life work the way you want it to.

It is now December 15...exactly five months since I began to write the book. I have not missed a single day and have written almost 200 vignettes to date. Of these, a majority will appear in the book you are now reading. Hopefully the daily mental messages/massages will motivate you to continue to invest in my forthcoming books and thus your personal development.

Make better use of the second greatest invention for learning, the written word. Read books, magazines, periodicals, biographies and anthologies on Success and Selling. Saturate your eyes and mind, and thereby your HEART, with any and all ideas designed to *increase your self-worth*...for as you think, so shall you earn! When I read a book, I annotate, underline and illustrate it in one color. When I reread the book, sometimes years later, I do the same thing, using a different color, thus enabling me to calibrate my personal growth, as I accept more ideas based on a continually evolving philosophy. I guess you'd say my personal success is color-coded for future reference.

9

# Two.

# Roses

When is a rose not a rose? When you're thinking about it. It becomes a rose in your mind when you begin to feel it's a rose. Let me explain. For many years I wanted to understand more about the relatively new science of hemisphericity, i.e., the brain and its bicameral functions. I attended a three-day session at the now defunct Tarrytown Conference Center just north of New York City. The highlight came on the last day, when our facilitator asked us to draw a rose. We all did, mostly with dismal results. Taking the best dozen drawings in the room I would still have hesitated to offer them to anyone I loved, unless I wanted to terminate the relationship at once. Imagine not finding 12 passable roses in a group of over 150 men and women.

Undaunted by the poor results, our facilitator now guided us into a long meditation, leaving our thinking brain (left side) behind. She led us into a forest of ROSES, with stems 30 feet tall. We then climbed into the rose itself, and we sat down. Next we began to inhale and smell the rose, then admire its color and texture. We were now using our feeling brain (right side) and the results were *startling* , almost *miraculous!* Almost the entire room now had roses on paper they could proudly give to loved ones. I kept mine for many years as a reminder to use my rational, linear brain a fraction of the time; instead I tap into my spatial, imaginative, intuitive, insightful and inspirational side more often.

The quality of your life will change in direct proportion to your right vs. left brain usage. If you can't stop to smell the flowers physically because of time restraints, you can always smell them in your mind. You'll feel refreshed when you do, and ready to tackle more mundane responsibilities than ever before.

Obviously this concept works in reverse for left-handers. Whenever I need a "fix" I mentally retire into my inner-space where time and space are not limited by science's measuring tools. When I come out, there are no longer problems ...just challenges and opportunities for personal growth.

Traveling inward for three short weeks can mean a different way of looking at things, and thus, a new and better way of life.

# Three

# The Souper Cooling Caper

This vignette has to do with change. Just as most of us are afraid of changing our ideas, so are we prone to leave things as they are...no matter how illogical or painful. A recent example comes to mind. For almost a decade I have watched my wife put an ice cube or two in her cup-a-soup to cool it off quickly. And for a decade I have smiled indulgingly, grateful that her idiosyncratic habit was truly harmless.

Yesterday I made myself a cup-a-soup, adding one packet of chicken flavored MBT for that extra kick I enjoy so much. The noodles were hot as usual. I was in a hurry and did not relish the thought of waiting for my soup to cool off...You guessed it! I added an ice cube, and it worked! I downed my soup, realizing I had a new weapon I could use to hasten my sumptuous feast. Since the ice cube comes from the same filtered water, my soup did not suffer taste-wise.

My wife is very logical and linear in her thinking, which is why I fought her idea for 10 years. When I think back of all the times I burned my tongue and palate trying to down hot soup I wonder from whom I inherited my stubborn streak. *But change I must or remain locked in an outdated past.* How's your Change Quotient? Do you resist change even when it's good for you? Look to your self-image if like me you are slow to change. All of our body cells change every 11 months. Except for our brain cells we have a completely new body every seven years. Perhaps our thinking should change at the same pace. Imagine having a new lifestyle every 7 years. That in itself would keep us from aging, as we spend much of our time getting ready for the next step in our personal growth...for change means growth.

I'm sure that I could learn a lot more if I watched my wife more carefully as she works her own timetable daily. I find that she wastes few motions as she takes care of the daily chores she has taken responsibility for. Unlike me, I can assure you. I gave up on time per se a long "time" ago. I believe life should go from accomplishment to accomplishment with little regard to the trivial periods in between. Making this philosophy work calls for a consummate diplomat, something I am still working on, since my belief can and does clash with my family's at times. (There goes that word again).

Now that I surrendered on the ice cube issue, I wonder what my next step forward will be? As you can see *there is hope for me yet*...and I am open to change. Perhaps I need to step up my pace a bit and not wait 10 years for each little victory over my ego. *P.S., my loving wife, in her wisdom, has never said to me: "Jacques, I told you so!"*

11

# *Four*

# Hate!

*"...and ye shall hate thy neighbor as thyself!"*

Ugly words, to be sure...and yet, they would certainly get our attention quicker than the wonderful command we are so familiar with. To tell the truth, most of us are keeping the hateful words as part of our daily philosophy. How else can we explain the shabby treatment we give so often to family, friends, neighbors and strangers? It is in effect a continuation of the shabby way we treat ourselves. Thus, hate begets hate!

The answer lies in *self forgiveness first*, and the forgiveness of others next. We must learn to forgive our self-hatred, which is based on fear, guilt and anger toward actions we committed or omitted in the past, which is over! Forgiveness comes easily once we have decided not to repeat the actions which caused the original anguish.

Then comes the more difficult part; forgiving all others! This includes the introverts, extroverts, ambiverts and perverts, and anyone who in your opinion hurt you physically, mentally or emotionally in any way. This may take in a very long list, since in most cases it will include our parents, siblings and peers first. Positive, forgiving affirmations used for 21 days should do the trick for most of us.

Sometimes the old habit comes back like a bad penny, and the hatred continues to pour forth. That's when the miracle of our mind takes over. We can immediately turn the thought around and send forgiveness once more...until the negative pull is gone forever. Then comes a great feeling called peace of mind!

Remember that self-hatred is closely tied to hatred for others. We must ever guard our minds to keep from separating the two, and work on them together.

Continue to hate, and you can expect illness upon illness to ravage your body and mind. "...as ye sew, so shall ye weep!" is what you'll attract.

The lack of forgiveness has given me the most trouble in my adult life. As a result I work on this positive quality continually. I have finally decided that most of the time I'm okay and you're okay. The trick now is to change the phrase most of the time to all of the time!

# *Five*

# In-Laws

I've got a problem with this topic. Not because of my in-laws, but because I've just realized that if I write about this subject I must also write about myself...as an In-Law! So where do I begin? With me or with the ones I've had in three different families?

I'll start with *me*...after all I've known *this* in-law longer than all the others put together. I believe I have finally become okay after many trials and errors. The trials on my in-laws and the errors mostly on my part. You see, I originally (33 years ago) thought in-laws were there for me to test my personal philosophies. When they resisted buying into my life style, I thought they were off the wall. Yet, when they tried to instill in me their traditions, I found that I too resisted. Was it just coincidence, or was there a message being passed on?

Fortunately, when things go awry in personal relationships I always do a bit of introspection. Guess what? That's when I find out I'm usually at least 50% to blame for this. After all I've been studying the human psyche since 1958, in one form or other. I should have gained some experience at dealing with my in-laws...be they parent, brother or sister.

One day, in heavy meditation...*eureka.!* The perfect formula came to me. I had this vision of gigantic red letters...and they formed an acronym, MYOB. What a revelation. Mind Your Own Business. It was as simple as that. Go into a left-brain mode; speak when spoken to, answer questions with a paucity of carefully chosen words, and most of all, *enjoy yourself* without trying to change anything.

When I first tested this idea, I almost bit my tongue off trying to keep from saying things that might only add to a problem. After several weeks my tongue healed and I no longer needed to bite it. I was cured. Now I have become the *great silent listener.* I can go for hours without saying anything, a mean feat for a professional speaker. But it's worth it, and that's what counts. It brings Peace of Mind at no cost to me.

The next time you're with your in-laws, try to remember that to *them* *you're* the in-law...and act accordingly. The rewards in lower stress and blood pressure are greater than the victory of possibly being right in something you said. My previous in-law attitude is now *outlawed*!

# TB - Terminal Boredom

"Go..............d, I'm bored!" "There's nothing to do in this house" "What a pain, living in this house!".......sound at all familiar? It probably does, if you have, or recently had a child, a teenager or a young adult living at home. I heard all three complaints within one hour uttered by siblings, ages 18, 14 and 9, living at home with their parents...who are friends of ours. Here they were, living in a middle class environment, with both parents working. The parents are both degreed, possess a library of hundreds of books, tapes, videos, etc...and the kids find *nothing to do*, and are bored to tears. I hear the same in my home with my teenager, but to a lesser degree.

I'm not sure about what parents and teachers are passing on to the next generation. The *love of learning* through *reading* is no longer on the priority list both home and schools used to have; of this I am sure.

Having been deprived of any education for 3 years as a refugee in North Africa, my mind became a sponge for knowledge. My *first week* in the United States I asked my aunt to take me to a library. I withdrew "The Count of Monte Christo" in the French edition, and began to read...read...read! I was 10 years old at the time, and no TV yet to interfere with my love for acquiring new knowledge...both fiction and non-fiction. I haven't stopped reading yet. I read on trains, planes, in diners, restaurants and bathrooms. You name it and I've probably read there. My son, whom I inherited at age 6 is not a reader. Just give him a stack of CDs, floor plans of new housing developments, and my wife and I don't see him for hours. Until he wants something that is. I don't fault him one bit, as he too is a victim of the system. I hurt for him at times, knowing how much more he would be able to offer of himself if he were a perennial reader. Terminal Boredom (our current epidemic of TB) is the cause of many maladjusted children and young adults, who end up misusing their logical, rational brain most of their lives. What they miss is the beauty and grandeur of dipping into the imaginative, highly creative right hemisphere, where all great inventions, discoveries and works of art (music, writing, sculptures, paintings, etc.) are produced.

You can lead a child to books, but you cannot make him read them. Leading by example works best if you catch the young mind at the crossroads...before it is too set in its ways. Work with your children as if their lives were at stake, for too often...they are!

# Seven

# T.L.C.

With three out of four mothers working outside the home these days and almost 25% of American children dropping out of high school each year, it is becoming more difficult than ever to treat the kids with the old formula...Tender, Loving Care.

Millions now live in one-parent homes, thus depriving them of the second parent on a full-time basis. More have become "latchkey" kids, wherein they must learn to fend for themselves most of the day. A majority of them will have been brought up by a single parent at some point in their childhood.

They have become for the most part, "rebels with a *cause*"...'*cause* nobody seems to give a damn anymore. Their suicide attempts run into the 100,000s, as they plead for more attention from those who gave them life. Grandparents no longer live with them as in the old days. They feel deserted...emotionally alone. We might call them "live-in orphans", the end results of a disposable-*products society*.

The old TLC is out of date, since it requires *time* at home with children to work properly. I'd like to suggest a new meaning to the old initials. I feel we can serve their cause better if we TLC them this way:

*Trust them, and let them know we do.*

*Love them, and show and tell that we do.*

*Competent...let them feel that they are competent!*

Since we already accept the fact that most Americans don't feel good about themselves, let us not pass this trait on to the next generation. If we do, they will pass it on to their next generation, and so on, and so on, etc....

Mental poverty is a far worse crime than material lacks. I came from a very poor home in Brussels, Belgium. My father, the last of nine children in Czechoslovakia, never saw his own father, who died before my dad was born. He had to work very early in life and never acquired a formal education. Yet he managed to instill in my brother and me a strong ethical code. Most of the problems I encountered in my life were a result of my disregard of what I had been taught in infancy. I have been reminded of his favorite saying, "Talk less and do more!" many times, and of its timeless wisdom. I have also learned not to suffer from premature articulation when speaking to the younger generation.

It never ceases to amaze me when I think of the different meanings the word "logic" has when it (logic) is used by people of a different generation. Sounds illogical, doesn't it?

# Eight

# Sex

My eyebrows shot up and across the room when I heard by 13 year old son lamenting his unfair fate. It seems a boy in his class had told him that he had just reached his sexual peak. To hear this at 13 can be quite traumatic. For once I was truly speechless. I could only mumble something about fairy tales. Anyhow, he has received new and improved information; it seems man's sexual peak is reached at 18...so now he has something to look forward to. As for me, I must have blinked when I was 18...for that age is only a "blur" in my memory.

Yes, I am for sex. Because of it I am here to write my story, and you are here to read it. But being for it does not condone 13 year olds already knowing too much about it! Will we ever stop pushing mature, R and X-rated data into the young minds of America? Or must they continue to receive information they are quite incapable of handling for many years to come? As teenagers they have enough confusion about their identities. Why mess with their sexuality and thus compound the problem of an already unsure and unstable ego.

I long for the old days when boys were boys, girls were girls and both were happy to be so, in no special hurry to grow up. Boys and girls became teenagers first, then grew into adulthood. We followed nature's call, and did things when it was time, and not when the advertising people decided we were to begin. I see 10 year olds with lipstick, painted fingernails, *smoking*, and trying to act much older. The operant word being trying...and failing. True maturity involves the ability to make intelligent decisions based on our own self worth...not someone else's opinion of us. Parents of today have a very tough time trying to rein in their children's unreasonable demands; the kids are always comparing themselves to the *others*. What they can have, do and be depends more and more on what they see advertised, both commercially and as "programming" on TV. Monkey see...and hear...and do has become a way of life for them, as major decisions are taken out of their hands (and minds). Thinking is left in the hands of professional manipulators who are only interested in *selling more goods!*

I spend a lot of time explaining this to my son with my fingers crossed, because I know parents today are fighting a lonely battle...waged against the children's *peers*. There are times I lose (not graciously, because so much is at stake); sometimes I win a small victory, and it gives me hope. Getting many As on a report card will only help partially in his quest for a healthy self-esteem. The rest must come as he learns that feeling good about himself is everything!

# Nine

# Patience

Patience...the ability to bear pain or trials calmly or without complaint. This is my dictionary definition of this much overworked word. Overworked these days because it is used so often when dealing with children, as well as immature adults.

I first learned the true meaning of patience when at age 18 I fractured the biggest bone in my body, my left femur (thigh bone). I was laid up for 13 weeks, strapped to my bed with ropes and weights. Then another 4 weeks in a wheelchair...and finally several weeks with crutches. All this on someone who had been on the high school track team earlier that year and who worked out with barbells 4 times per week. Need I say more?

Patience became my middle name. As soon as I understood that I would be immobile for *months* I had to decide on a new attitude. This was before TV in the wards, which eliminated one major source of escape. Radio interfered with other patients so that had to be used sparingly. I was left with the choice of staring at the old hospital ceiling or starting to read on a regular basis. I began to read voraciously, a habit I have not given up. Not only did I have to cultivate *patience* while incapacitated as a patient many years ago, but need it currently as well. I need patience while waiting for planes to take off; waiting for taxis and limos to pick me up as I travel from city to city doing one-day seminars. I need patience while waiting for my wife when I take her to lunch on Wednesdays and dinner on Saturdays. I especially need patience when dealing with my son, who is now 15, and knows *everything*.

I may have paid a high price to learn my lesson; I hope today's teenagers have it easier. I said hope, not believe. Since all problems developed on TV seems to be solved in 30 minutes or one hour, minus announcements (no more commercials, you'll note) today's kids have developed *impatience* to unheard of levels. They can't wait to grow up. They'll start to smoke and drink and use drugs as soon as peer pressure is strong enough. Can't wait to get the car, test their plumbing with the opposite sex, leave home, etc...

Patiently, I wait for this once great nation to get its priorities in order again. Children are the future, yet their present looks very bleak. Whenever I have the opportunity I discuss this with my audiences, whether on TV, radio or at lectures. I do this because of my deep respect for our children's *untapped potential*, and because they will lead our nation in the future. A final, soul-searching question. Are you part of the problem, or the solution?

# *Ten*

# Affirmations

The main question you may have at this time is: Do they work? The answer is a resounding yes! Not only do they work, they have been working in *your life* for many years! Want proof? Get yourself a golf scorer (looks like a watch, complete with band) and start clicking away each time you affirm something, whether verbally or silently to yourself.

Examples of affirmations include the following:

I knew I would mess this up...I'm incapable...I told you I couldn't do it...I hate myself when I...I can't...I'm not able...I'm clumsy...I'm stupid...I'm not good enough...I should have done...I'll never be able to...I'm too short...too fat...too ugly...etc....

Surprised yourself, didn't you? Bet you thought all this time that affirmations are *positive* things you say to yourself. Affirmations are simply affirmations. They solidify and make *real* any thought or idea you have, both Positive or *Negative*. If you followed directions and used the golf scorer you would be *shocked* at the number of <u>*negative affirmations*</u> you make on a daily basis. Hopefully the number will be under 100 per day...but don't put your money on it.

To paraphrase..."as a person thinketh in his heart, so is he!" To think in one's heart is to *feel*...(the Bible had no word for Feelings) and what you think and feel and *affirm*, so will you be/become.

The beauty of affirmations is that you can control them, once you are aware of them as being just that. Negatives will breed negatives, and positives will therefore breed positives. You can choose how you want your life lived by what you say, think and feel. How's that for a great gift from our Creator?

Just as you can stop a child from crying by tickling him, so can you immediately change a negative into a positive...by just deciding to do so. The power to *choose* is ours to use or misuse. The results are predictable. To repeat, "as ye sow, so shall ye reap!"

*Choose* peace of mind, harmony, success, love...whatever turns you on, and affirm daily...affirm...affirm...until this too becomes second nature to you, as were the negatives in your past. Negatives belong in a photographer's studio, not in God's greatest miracle, your mind.

# Eleven

# Intalk

Intalk is one of the words I hope makes its way into the dictionary someday. I thought it would compliment words like insight, intuition, inspiration...since they all represent a skill which manifests from the inside out. Intalk is generally activated from within, yet it is a result of outside influences. Intalk is when either or both sides of the brain is/are engaged in mental conversation. When both sides are dialoguing they use the corpus callosum as a communication center. It is composed of over 200 million brain cells, and can transmit millions of impulses at once when necessary.

My question now becomes...with such an incredibly powerful bio-computer ready to do our bidding at a moment's notice...why are most of the intalking conversations we have of a negative nature? Why do we abuse God's greatest gift to us and continue to fill our brain with nonsense? Pessimism in the U.S. is at its highest level, and continues to grow at a faster rate than does our population.

According to Isaac Asimov the average brain consists of over 100,000,000,000 (yes, that's billions) cells with interconnecting links going into the Trillions. Experts estimate that to duplicate one brain we would need a computer 100 stories tall, and the size of Texas. Yet all this potential is contained in in this mini-universe weighing just three pounds. Perhaps we should consider re-cycling our brains and see if we could make better use of it the second time around, or we could just decide to re-think what we are doing with it this time. The *only* difference between the Optimist and the Pessimist is how they decide to *process* the input they receive, and thus control their intalk. In computer talk...garbage in, garbage out (GIGO) has long been understood. Why can't we realize the same rules apply when we analyze incoming facts and figures. The "garbage" will go into the mental "garbage bin" and the "good" stuff in the "good" bin. For example...if you listen at night to bad news (95% of all news) you will go to bed with your mind on "garbage". The same applies to mornings; listen to the news first thing and you can predict a pretty negative morning at work.

Here's an obvious suggestion which works! Fill your mind with *Posimins* (another one of my newly coined words) meaning Positive Vitamins...and watch your attitude change! If you control what goes into your head you will control your intalk as well, and not have it control you. Control your brain and you control your destiny!

# Twelve

# Faith

.....as ye sow, so shall ye reap!

Two young priests, John and Mark meet after their first sermons in adjacent towns. John asks Mark: "How did you make out with the collection?" Mark replies: "Fine. Most parishioners put in folded money. How did you do?" John replies: "Not so good, and I don't understand. I put in a coin to start the offerings and all I got was small change. How much did you put in your basket?" "A five dollar bill", replied Mark.

The subject of faith is very tricky I find. We have unlimited faith in complete strangers, such as gas station attendants, waiters and restaurant cooks, airplane pilots, car salesmen and insurance reps...yet!...when it comes to God and the promise that we are made in God's image we fail miserably. We believe the gas station attendant when he tells us he is pouring diesel in our tank; we trust the waiters and cooks to prepare and deliver fresh, clean and edible food. We accept that the airplane pilot is not drunk, knows our destination. We believe the car salesman and purchase our second largest investment based on this stranger's recommendation. Finally we put our faith into insurance people and sign documents only the CIA could decipher successfully. We print "In God We Trust" on our monies. Perhaps that's the problem. Since the money is now worth a fraction of its original face value, perhaps we should reprint it to say instead: "In God We Trust 20% Of The Time!" At least that's how we live these days. We pray on Moody Mondays, Tired Tuesdays, Worrisome Wednesdays, Thoughtless Thursdays, Fearful Fridays, Slow Saturdays and Sunny (?) Sundays. We beg, plead, cajole, and cry, trying to overturn the original law of Cause and Effect. Mr. Robert Muller, Assistant Secretary-General of the U.N., tells us that there are no less than 5,000 world religions, with 25,000 subordinate branches thereof. And yet they all agree that..."as a person thinketh in his heart so is he!" Change your feelings and you change your mind and attitude. And thus regain control of your lie. Remember the sequence: ...in God we trust...we are made in God's image...we can thus trust ourselves.

I truly believe that: *The travel we do on the road inward gives us the best mileage in life!*

# *Thirteen*

# Ego

I find that wherever Igo, Ego...! Whenever I'm asked at my seminars to pinpoint mankind's greatest problem, the answer I give is always the same as is the solution. I tell my attendees that working with our "false ego is the problem, and leaving it at home is the solution." I know this is easier said than done, especially if we have been building up this ego (i.e., persona) for a period of many years. It becomes more and more difficult to dislodge as we add more psychological bricks to shore it up, and to hide our true selves behind. Because the ego needs constant defending from outside stimuli we tend to go on the offense (pun intended). This includes condemning and criticizing others so that their attention is focused away from us. Another mental game we play to avoid being on the receiving end is to complain. Since most people will not attack someone who is down this tactic keeps us from becoming the butt of others' criticism and condemnation. Either way, we use these techniques to keep the world away from our feelings.

If instead we changed our feelings by developing a strong and healthy self-image, we could then look at the outside world without being threatened by what we see. If we took the word ego and made an acronym designed to remind us daily how to accomplish the above, this is what it might look like:

E - for Enthusiasm (God residing within us).

G - for Goals, new ones based on Enthusiastic Self-Worth.

O - for Optimism, as we go after our Goals with Enthusiasm!

The best method of self-help is through affirmations. Something we have been doing all our lives, much to our detriment. As you have probably guessed, affirmations come in two sizes; negative and positive. Negative affirmations are the self-condemnations we use when someone has attacked our ego, thus reinforcing our poor self-image. No less a world authority than Albert Einstein has told us that it takes 11 positives to eliminate one negative. If we can believe one of the greatest scientists who ever lived, we need to use 11 positive affirmations just to get our mind back into *neutral*; then, a twelfth affirmation is necessary to put us into a healthy ego state. For example, saying "I can't do this" is an affirmation with a negative root. So is "I'll try to do this", because it presupposes the possibility of defeat. Instead, "I can do it" or "I've done tougher things in the past" are positive ways to program our minds toward a successful solution. All it takes is *practice, practice, practice, practice, practice, practice,* ad infinitum...I think you get the message!

# Fourteen

# Pithecanthropus Stegosaurus

Sometimes I think the above title would best describe man as he is today (man as in mankind). Why? Because like the antediluvian animal named Stegosaurus I believe we also possess two brains...a very small one in the head and a much larger one in our "tail" (i.e., derriere). This means that too often we *act* much faster than we *think*--a la Stegosaurus. As a result we end up confusing Activity with Accomplishment...ergo much motion but very little progress. We all know what eventually happened to this two-brained animal; I certainly hope our fate is kinder. If you want to see what an extinct species looks like go to the Washington National Museum; you'll notice there is plenty of room for "extinct" man to stand next to the Stegosaurus. Reader's Digest, with its monthly circulation of over 31 million subscribers worldwide told us that our interests are--by order of importance:

1 - My Health...2 - My Wealth...3 - My Self-Improvement...4 - My Marriage and 5 - My Desire to Get Ahead.

Seems to me as though we are a bit Myopic in our view of the world. Once again we are guilty of "backward" thinking...which the results verify. There is nothing wrong with wanting health, wealth, a good marriage and a successful career. What's wrong with this picture is that we put *self-improvement* in the middle of our dreams and desires--and yet this is the only one listed which can help us to attain the others. This is simply butt-thinking. Instead the need is to concentrate on improving the self...which is the cornerstone of our life and its ultimate accomplishments.

Self-improvement is deeply rooted in virtuous ethics--as taught by Aristotle, Plato, Augustine, Kant, Mill and many others who understood its value in personal development. According to the Boston Globe 3 out of 4 high school students admit to cheating; in college the number is 1 out of 2. Also, 34% of these college-age students said they would steal from their employer. Only 6% of the people over 45 years old would admit this gross breach of trust. Obviously erosion does not occur on land only. There has been a continuing pattern of *moral erosion* in our nation since the advent of the "boob" tube which invades our homes without monitoring its content. Still accepting that we'll believe it when we see it we absorb the prodigious output of this new god (in whom we trust) as if it were the gospel for the '90's.

Perhaps the apple does not fall far from the tree; but if it lies on the ground and is not nurtured immediately it begins to decay, eventually to rot. Morality these days has a high rate of mortality. Self-improvement works when we get out of the current gray area of ethical behavior, back to solid black and white values.

# Fifteen

# Rent -A - Anything

In 1988, I had the honor of addressing a convention celebrating the 25th anniversary of a rent-anything company. It was a three-day affair, in January. You know I was very glad to be in Miami, Florida at that time of year. After my keynote speech to 400 attendees I spent the rest of the day walking through their "exhibition hall". True to their name they rented out everything; well, almost everything. They stayed away from the world's oldest profession (although Miami supplied those in amplitude for anyone interested) and also did not have a Rent-A-Mourner or Rent-A-Friend. These new needs are now supplied by California firms. Imagine having lived a lifetime, dying and then needing rented mourners to help your transition from this world to wherever God's travel agent has booked.....Or, you're in a hospital and have to rent friends so that you won't be alone during visiting hours.

Since we are more populated than ever we are not alone. Lonelier than ever, yes...but not alone. Loneliness is not a physical problem; it comes from our inner world of feelings.

If "Mourners 'R Us" and "Friends 'R Us" sound like an inhumane way to earn a living, let's remember that these new "products" are filling a need. Speaking of which, the thought that "people who need people are the luckiest people in the world" is truly neurotic. The trick is not to need people but to like being with them. If we need outside stimulus in order to feel good about ourselves, life is passing us by...and we will need to rent-a-friend or mourner. If however, we turn inward and become our own best friend first...we will then attract friends from the outside, for "like attracts to like". In my sales training sessions I teach that clients will buy from people who most "resemble" them psychologically. That's why NLP (Neuro-Linguistic-Programming) is fast becoming the science for the '90s. It's also known as the do-do philosophy. As they do, so you do. By thus becoming an alter ego to the prospect (or friend) we make it easy and business deals are often formed using this simple method. Of course it means subjugating our ego and conforming to theirs temporarily. An easy feat if your self-esteem is healthy.

Perhaps Rent-A-Love is an idea who time has come. If we rent love long enough it could easily become a habit. We all know habits are very tough if not impossible to break. I'd love to visit a store whose marquee read: Lovers 'R Us. Pleas let me know when one opens up in your area. I have enough bonus points from American Airlines to see it.

# Sixteen

# "Odd Couples"

I was watching a re-re-re-run of "The Odd Couple", when a brilliant lightbulb went off in my head...known as an idea! As the heat from the light cooled down, I started to think about other instances of my newly-born thought. They came rather quickly, in the form of several TV successes. Here's what I mean. We have the dynamic "duos" Felix Unger and Oscar Madison (The Odd Couple); Christine Cagney and Mary Beth Lacey (Cagney and Lacey); Sam Malone and Diane Chambers (Cheers); and finally, Edith and Archie Bunker (All in the Family). I can name many more, but the point will be made with the above examples.

The human brain is bi-cameral, having two separate "chambers", each housing a hemisphere. The left side is usually the rational, thinking part of the brain. The right side is the intuitive, feeling part. Now, go back to the TV programs outlined above, and a strange coincidence (?) occurs in all of them. The show producers have pitted a "left-brainer" against a "right-brainer" in each instance...and it works! They are always fighting and disagreeing with each other, which makes for great conflict or comedy...both highly desirable commodities on TV. This brings me back to the human condition. If our hemispheres are not working synergistically toward a common goal, there is much conflict, and very little comedy. In other words, much of our personal frustrations are a result of left-brain fighting right-brain. These disagreements between the rational and the intuitive ...or the thinking vs. feeling we experience, often will cause undue stress on our immune system and bring on psychosomatically, self-induced illness.

Understanding this, it behooves us to do what the Greeks told us over two millenia ago: *Know Thyself!* Only then will we be able to become fully functioning beings, living in a stress-free society. To put this another way; if what you think and feel do not work well together, you must change your thoughts or your feelings until both agree. Easier said than done! One way I found of doing this is to make two lists...on paper... List A enumerates my thoughts on a subject, and list B gives me my feelings by the numbers. I then match the lists, making the necessary changes.

We are all, in effect, an "odd couple" in the head. Left brain gets its input from outside stimuli; right brain is born with "intuitive" knowledge. If ever they are to cooperate, ego (i.e., left-side) must subordinate itself to the right (correct) side...the Inspirational one. Inspirational meaning the spirit residing within.

# Seventeen

# Nature

It is 7 A.M. I am sitting in my living room enjoying the morning rays streaming through the vertical blinds. As usual, when I'm not meditating, I'm thinking, and looking at the two plants growing in the room. The most striking feature of both plants is their constant proliferation. They never stand still. The weak leaves die and fall away. The strong get stronger, forming a permanent nucleus around which the life/death struggle takes place. This never-ending cycle reminds me of the human brain. As we grow and mature, our weak ideas die, to be replaced by younger and stronger ones. Psychologists tell us we are bombarded daily by over 60,000 stimuli, many of which are new ideas. If we don't grab some of them and work on them, they join our gigantic mental graveyard which is comprised of our old memories, feelings and discarded ideas.

I also noticed that my plants take full advantage of their environment, using their full potential, limited only by the amount of water and space allotted to them. This is where the analogy ends, much to our loss. The newest available information on human potential (Stanford U. Human Resources Dept.) tells us we use 2% of our full abilities on a daily basis. Unlike the plants, we do not take full advantage of our natural, bountiful gifts. Instead, most of us work with a fixed set of ideas all of our lives, rarely, if ever, changing the direction of our thinking. A good example might be someone driving an automobile with the right foot on the gas and the left on the brake...*at the same time* ...and taking the same route every day. No wonder doctors have come up with yet another disease, and named it CFS...Chronic Fatigue Syndrome. Putting brakes on God's greatest gift, the human brain, will surely wreak havoc with our insides, both physical and mental.

When speaking of nature, my thoughts are simple: First, don't mess with nature, and second...go with the flow. An easy rule to follow might also be: If it feels right (gut-wise), it usually is right, for hunches come from the right hemisphere, which connects directly via red phone to Infinite Intelligence.

The weather will continue as is whether we bitch about it or not. Yet, many of us will allow it to spoil our day's activities because it (the weather) chooses not to follow our designs for it. Let us instead bend to the will of nature, and be flexible enough to alter our plans in a way compatible with the happenings outside of our homes and offices. This will surely diminish our daily stress level, and allow us to "leave home without it!" (The tranquilizers, that is).

25

# *Eighteen*

# Spiritual Vacuum

The latest polls show that as a nation, we are operating in a spiritual vacuum. For example, we have less trust than ever in our government officials, big business and especially, the fourth estate...the media, including television and daily newspapers. The ethical standards championed by our Judeo-Christian heritage have gone the way of the dinosaurs, extinct, and buried deep in the ground. Morality has given way to *mortality* where ethical conduct is concerned.

Although I am the eternal optimist, I feel that I am becoming part of an old and even smaller minority who still believe in the ultimate goodness of humanity. Science is moving at such a crazy pace, that it boggles the mind to try and keep up with the new products heaped on us almost daily. The logical, thinking, rational brain is reeling from this scientific assault, and the results are stress, frustration and much hidden anger.

The answer of course lies in a renaissance of feeling rather than all this rationalization via linear thinking. We seem to be suppressing our intuitive goodness by relegating it to a "back burner" in our mind. If SELF-expression is still one of our main goals in life, it behooves us to really understand this Self. By shutting off our senses for a short period of time each day, we can begin slowly to regain our initial enthusiasm (the God residing within us) for living. I found that when *medication* is replaced by *meditation,* my psychoneuroimmunological (now there's a mouthful) system begins to work in my favor, and life regains its original charm for me. By meditation, I do not mean sitting naked, concentrating on my navel...Anything that stills the outer (left) mind will do the trick. Just resting or listening to quieting music, (baroque is excellent for this) looking at a peaceful scene, whether live or painted, or just contemplating our inner feelings, are all good meditative techniques that work.

Any method of self--discipline will help to fill the spiritual vacuum many of us are suffering from. You will then find that the humorous "11th commandment" which says: "Thou shalt not pill", can become your new philosophy where your health is concerned. Psychoneuroimmunology dictates that health always begins in the *mind,* travels through the neuro (*nervous*) system and ends on strengthening the *immune* (fighter) cells in the body.

Unless you can come up with a workable explanation for the miracle of the body/mind connection, I will continue to believe there is Infinite Intelligence at work within each of us...until we choose to interfere with it...using our *limited* intelligence. "Physician heal thyself" must be changed to ".....(your name here) heal thyself!

# Nineteen

# The Red Phone

We all have a red phone. Not the famous one which taps into the White House for emergencies. Ours is settled in our right brain, frontal lobe, and it is connected to the White Light...or to the Creator, or Universal Intelligence, or God or any other name you're most comfortable with. The fact remains that atheists cannot explain the Universe satisfactorily. Anyhow, this red phone we own rent-free is located near the greatest communications center in the world...the corpus colassum, which consists of over 200 million connecting lines. The trick to activating the phone, and thus the god within us (Enthusiasm), is to connect our thinking brain (left) with our feeling side (right) where we have access to intuition, insight, inspiration and the innate wisdom of the ages.

To dial this Super Intelligence, we need only "still" the rational, linear part of our mind. There are many disciplines one can use to cause the inner stillness. There is meditation, great music from the mental giants of the past, visualizations, hatha yoga, mantras, etc...The method for connecting is not important. *Intent* is. Once the turbulent brain is at rest, the messages begin to arrive through the red phone. If we listen to them, and follow their advice, we will be in much greater control of our lives. These messages are known as "hunches".

Try a 21 day test. Listen to your hunches and follow them to the letter. After this short test, for the next 21 days, listen, but do not follow the ideas. Watch what happens, and match the results of both 3-week tests. I know you'll be much happier with what happened in your first test. If you discontinue using your magnificent message center...check your self-image. Find out why you don't feel worthy of a much better and easier way to live. Then, work on that!

It is also okay to use your red phone for giving thanks to the advice giver.

When I forget my red phone, I usually step into "it". See if it works for you in the same way. I ignore the phone when my ego wants to be the boss over my life and actions, and I pay the price. I pay...and I pay...and I pay. I'm sure you understand.

# Twenty

# Early Birds

Sometimes the early bird does not get the worm. Instead, it may get "wormed" out of a job. Here's what happened yesterday when I called up a high school for which I was doing a lecture on developing a healthier self-esteem.

-Hello, could I speak with Mrs.....please? This is Mr. Weisel calling.

-I'm sorry sir, but Mrs.....just left for the day.

-Really! What hours can I reach her at her office?

-She works from 9 to 3.

-Is that right? Well, it's only a quarter to three.

-Yes, she works until three, so she leaves at a quarter to three.

*She works until three, so she leaves at a quarter to three?*

Did I hear that correctly? If I did, this is one of the best examples of *convoluted thinking* I have ever run across. Is it any wonder we are losing the battle for world commerce.

I watch immigrants come to the U.S. as I did in 1943, during World War II. They don't speak the language, yet, in a few short years, manage to own businesses and are able to send their children to the finest universities. Not knowing English when they came over, they did not know that today in the U.S. you try to work as little as you can get away with. Last night I gave a lecture to the Personnel Society of Long Island. I asked one of the personnel managers of a very large company: "How many people do you have working for your company?" "About half of them", he answered. A joke, perhaps...but a bitter one in today's workplace. An also-ran bit of humor goes like this: "When did she first start to work for you?" The answer: "When I threatened to fire her!"

To be a productive member of society is like carrying a lifetime passport to a strong self-image. The benefits of doing a job well are better health as well as financial returns. It gives purpose to an otherwise dull life, and helps us to get up in the morning because we feel we have something important to contribute to the day ahead.

It is a fact that work actually *frees us*, as we can then truly enjoy our off-time, because we feel we have *earned it!* The Bible tells us in Thessalonians, "If any would not work, neither should he eat". Work separates humanity from the rest of the living creatures *only* by its nature. After all, we know that ants and bees work much harder than we ever would, but at a much lower level of accomplishment. Let us not give **40%** of our workday to the company (**USA Today** survey of 3,000 employees across the United States), but instead give 110%...and we will never worry about having a place to report daily.

28

# Twenty One

# Judge Not, lest...

The Scene: The Jacksonville Fla., Airport.
The Players: A young lady and an elderly gentleman.
The Time: Both waiting for a delayed flight.

The story begins when the lady buys a magazine and a box of cookies at the airport, intending to read and nibble while she waits for her late flight to arrive. She sits down and puts her belongings on the tray separating her seat from the above-mentioned gentleman. As she starts to read her magazine, he reaches into the box of cookies and takes one. She takes one...and he takes one again. As she continues to eat the cookies, he keeps right up with her, until there is only one left. He picks it up, breaks it in half, and gives one to the lady. By this time she is so furious with him, she gets up and walks away, giving him a "look that could kill". He meanwhile is gently smiling at her.

The final scene takes place as she gets ready to board the plane and rummages through her carry-on for her ticket. In order to reach her ticket, she has to remove *her box of cookies*. End of story perhaps...but not of what happened. As I now understand it, when we judge anyone, we are really judging ourselves. "Judge not since you judge *yourself!*" is the way it should be rephrased. That alone would cut down on the times we "judge" others, since it would really mirror our inadequacies--thus *reinforcing* them. I truly believe we do too much of this daily...as we self-talk our way into a bigger inferiority complex each time we finish the words, "I am..." with a negative statement. Instead, it is recommended that we use the *I am's* with positive feedback so that a healthy self-concept emerges as a result of this highly personal "intalk". Telling ourselves we are worthy of love, admiration, friends and success will help smooth over the rough terrain we often find in front of us as we travel through life.

To the best of my current ability, I accept people as they are...and let them decide on any changes needed to improve their lives. For example, as a motivational speaker, *I do not motivate* anyone; instead I offer options for them to think about. Any resultant change comes because the person decided it would benefit him/her to do so. My sole responsibility is to show that we don't have to stay average or mediocre, and to explain what works in my life. Babies never complain about having fat thighs or double chins. They grow up non-judgmental...until someone comes along and screws up their thinking, injecting them with intellectual garbage from which many of them never recover. *Be careful!*

# Twenty Two.

# The Power of Love

If your thoughts run along the line of "I'm not good enough", rather than "I am a valuable human being", something important was left out of your early years. Feeling valuable is one of the two legs holding up your personality. The other leg, of course, represents the degree of love given to you during the formative years. If one leg is shorter than the other, your "jog" through life will be very shaky as you run with uneven legs.

Dr. M. Scott Peck, in his classic book "The Road Less Traveled", writes: "When children have learned through the love of their parents to feel valuable, it is almost impossible for the vicissitudes of adulthood to destroy their spirit". A very powerful message, not to be taken lightly. Therefore, if you did not get the proper stroking and nurturing (9 out of 10 did not), you must immediately do two things. First, *forget the negative past*, and second, forgive your parents who after all, did their best, although that fell short of *your* emotional needs.

Recently, some interesting data re: Love and its impact on life was revealed in a study of male adults who suffered a heart attack. The strongest and most important factor in the recovery of those who lived was that they felt they were *loved* by their wives. Those who felt unloved by their spouses, tended to die. This emotional need superseded their lifestyles, including diet, exercise, smoking and even the will to live. This is why I feel very strongly that love should be a "show and tell" fixture in the home. It means that we must show that we love, and say so on a daily basis. I believe we need "soul food" as well as body food in order to maintain homeostasis (healthful balance).

If love was lacking in our childhood, we must begin to learn to love ourselves. The keys to positive change include a program of *self-acceptance* and *self-approval*. When we truly learn to love ourselves, we will have both feet on the ground, holding up legs of equal length (love and value). At this point, our walk through life will be one of pleasure and profit. Remembering that every thought, spoken or unspoken, helps create our future, it behooves us to watch what we think all day long. When you change a *thought,,* you change the *feeling* attached to it. That's why I always recommend changing negative affirmations to positives as they occur. The option to make these changes does come from within; to paraphrase a Con Edison slogan..."Dig you must for a cleaner you!" I agree with Carl Jung when he says that if your life isn't working right by age 35, there is a spiritual vacuum (my term) which needs to be worked out. Remember that you were given dominion over all on earth; this includes you, but the decision to take charge of your life must come from *within*.

# Twenty Three

# Prayer

There is an apocryphal story which goes like this: A young priest writes to his bishop asking for permission to smoke while he prays. "Absolutely not!" is the emphatic reply from the bishop. A few days later, another priest from the same parish writes to the bishop asking if he could pray while he smokes. This time the reply is also emphatic: "Of course you may, my son!" Obviously, how you approach the subject of prayer is very important.

The reason prayers don't work for millions of people is not very difficult to understand. They pray for things not to happen to them. They're afraid of ill health, poverty, romantic loss and other *negative* things happening to them. The operant word here is happening; and what we concentrate on will *happen*! If they turned their attention to what they *wanted* instead of what they hoped to *avoid*, the end result would literally startle them. This is part of the sewing/reaping syndrome, wherein we get what we most concentrate on.

Prayer works best when one is doing something worthwhile with his/her life. Then the work *is the prayer* and there is little need to ask for good things to happen. The work itself will attract what you most want. Not getting what we want brings on guilt feelings, which in turn, perpetuate the need to pray for things not happening to us.

We need to learn to focus on the things that will make us happier and more productive as human beings. We know that tens of millions of Americans are continually on some diet or other. The psychologists also tell us that over 90% of the diets we follow fail to do the job. Main reason...once again we concentrate on the negative aspect of the diet, i.e., losing weight. Instead, if we work on becoming thinner, healthier and more attractive, the human meltdown would begin automatically, with positive results.

The motive to prayer must be couched in affirmative language if you expect (and expect you must) things to improve on a permanent basis. Motive must come from the heart...not the mind, if it is to influence what you pray for.

To pray is to implore, to beseech...to beg for! I believe begging should be left for beggars. If we truly have been given dominion over this planet and all its living things, we do not need to beg for what is already ours!

The great Lebanese poet, Kahlil Gibran (1883-1931), wrote in his "On Prayer":

"You pray in your distress and in your need; would that you might pray also in the fullness of your joy and in your days of abundance."

# Twenty Four

# Racism

As a World War II refugee, I have felt the brunt of racism in several countries. When my family and I ran from the Nazis in 1940, we ended up in a small French village, Villaries. I was only 7 years old, and had to run home from school because my schoolmates wanted to see my "horns". One month later, we ran again. We landed in Casablanca, Morocco, where we stayed as displaced persons until the Allies invaded 2 1/2 years later. This time the Arab and French kids made life miserable for my brother and me. In the U.S. I've run into racism in New York, as well as some of the many states I visited as a speaker.

Based on my past experiences, as well as a continuing search for the right answers, here are some thoughts on racism.

According to educators who specialize in children, the first five years are more important in attitude-training than any other 5-year period in their lives. This means that before children enter kindergarten, they have already acquired values, basic skills and a sense of self-worth...positive or negative. This is also commonly referred to as Self-Esteem, something which less than 10% of the population has in adequate amounts. The reasons are myriad, but the one constant in all the major research remains the home, and what happens during the formative years. After querying over 7,000 seminar attendees last year, the high majority agreed that the reason they did not feel good about themselves is because of the mixed signals their parents gave them, resulting in a poor or low self-esteem, and a low self-esteem is at the root of all racism. In January 1989, a nationwide study was made by the Carnegie Foundation for the Advancement of Teaching. Of the 22,000 teachers polled, 90% of them felt a lack of parental support was a problem in their schools. My most recent source of information is the book published in January 1990, called "Toward A State of Esteem", which details an extensive 3-year program called "California Task Force to Promote Self-Esteem". This volume will probably remain the definitive work on the subject for many years to come. Its basic recommendations with reference to education and self-esteem include:

a - educate every educator through pre-service and in-service training in self-esteem and responsibility.

b - promote more parent involvement.

c - implement programs to counteract bigotry and prejudice.

A perfect example of locking up the barn after the horse is stolen.

# Twenty Five

# Fingerling Fish-Fry

We all know that fishermen tell tall tales. Well, here's a short one instead. It seems two friends were out fishing together, and one of them kept throwing back into the lake the nice, large fishes he caught, and kept the fingerlings. When asked about this by his friend, he replied: "I have to throw the large ones back, since I only have an 8-inch frying pan."

Do you have an 8-inch frying pan located in your head, so that you have to throw back any idea larger than that back into the universe? According to Dr. Burton White, (author of "The First Three Years of Life") not more than one child in ten gets off to a proper start in the United States. One of the main reasons for this indictment is that as children, we often develop a personality by kowtowing to those we come most often in contact with. In order to make and keep friends, we follow sheep-like those whose opinions of us are more important to our esteem than our own!

There is nothing wrong with emulating others...if they are people who will *enrich our life.* In parts of Switzerland, canaries are trained to sing beautifully by being caged together with nightingales when they are very young. Much nicer than the other famous story which says that if you go to bed with dogs, you'll get up with fleas. The associations you make in your life will determine to a great extent whether you'll flourish or perish as a conditioned human being. One of the key factors in our early development is centered on the expectation others have of us. Studies in the 1970's, and reinforced in the 1980's, show a definitive relationship between expectations and outcomes.s This means we have a personal obligation to choose wisely, those who would teach us...since teachers' predictions can become self-fulfilling prophecies.

The same holds true for our parents who are our original teachers. What they *expect* of us we *accept* as gospel, and proceed to do as we are programmed. Both teachers and parents need to understand the power they wield in influencing their charges, and they can make or break us, based on their attitudes toward us. The teachers who love to teach and the parents who love their children, will make it their business to instill only positive data to those they are responsible for.

When a young child goofs, it is important for the adult dealing with the problem to separate the wrongful action from the person responsible for it. Judge and reprimand the act, never the child.

You will feel little love for yourself if you cannot pass love along to those who need your guidance in order to mature.

# Twenty Six

## -8-

The figure "8" in this case stands for a continuous loop. The loop I refer to is the circuitous treadmill many of us call ours, as we proceed on a daily basis to repeat...peat...peat...peat...the pattern of our lives. We hang on to this treadmill as if our existence depends on it. Reminds me of the grizzly bears one encounters in our national parks. One such grizzly once came upon a campfire with a cauldron of soup on it. The hungry bear, smelling the soup, decided this was for him. He quickly lifted the scalding hot container, hugged it to his chest and began to walk away with his treasure. The cauldron began to burn his chest, and true to his nature, the bear gave it a mighty "bear hug" in order to render his new enemy senseless. The harder he squeezed, the more he burned himself and the angrier and more frustrated he became.

And that's how a majority of Americans go through life...squeezing their anger and frustration ever so closer to their heart, or lifeline. No wonder we succumb by the millions to all sorts of ailments, and need over 60 million prescriptions per annum for tranquilizers, not counting the billions of dollars spent on drugs. Drugs and tranquilizers do not cure, they only *relieve* some of the hundreds of symptoms now catalogued in the medical journals.

No wonder doctors don't make house calls. They would have to replace the old black leather bag with two trunks full of sedatives, placebos and other paraphernalia to satisfy the fickle patients they serve. According to a prominent physician, that little black leather bag contained 90% of the relief sought by the ill. If the human body is our Creator's greatest miracle, why does it require thousands of different drugs for proper maintenance. Why, the lowly automobile requires less and can survive us as well. There are antique cars on the road over 100 years old, and one Mercedes diesel (1957) has clocked almost 1,200,000 miles as I write this. Now that's staying power.

Aeschylus (525-456 B.C.) wrote the following: "Words are the physician of a mind diseased". He understood that the body will respond to what's troubling the mind and cause appropriate illness in the body, and that the cure lies in the mind. When you don't feel well, don't ask yourself, "What's wrong with me?"...Instead ask, "Who's wrong with me?", because the quickest cures result when we get rid of a psychological problem, fueled by anger, hatred or frustration at someone (including the self).

To truly love yourself means to heal yourself, without the need for narcotics or other means. "Health that mocks the doctor's rules, knowledge never learned of schools." This from Whittier, preeminent American poet who died 100 years ago.

# Twenty Seven

# P.A.R.E.N.T.S.

I love to use acronyms, since they serve a great purpose when giving a lecture or seminar. They are mnemonic devices, used as mental triggers to move the presentation ahead in the right direction without the need for extensive notes. Each letter leads into a one to five minute presentation. For example, the word "parents" has seven letters, which means I can plan for a seven to thirty-five minute talk, depending on the current time frame I would work under. Instead, I'll use the acronym for a vignette, hoping some of the parents reading this will use the thoughts behind the letters when dealing with their offspring.

The letter "P" stands for Patience, without which all is lost when trying to communicate with children. It is the most difficult to internalize...but well worth cultivating. "P" is also the beginning of Praise, something we give too little of.

"A" is for my favorite word, Attitude...which makes everything go *for* or *against* you, depending on what attitude you have when spending time with family. "A" is also Appreciation, which you must not be skimpy with. Apply liberally and watch the results.

The next letter, "R", represents the Respect you must show to your kids, no matter what age they are. Conversely, they must show respect to you as well. Respect must be earned by both sides, yours and theirs, and cannot be force-fed intravenously like food which the kids may detest.

Following the "R" is the letter "E", which prefaces the word Ego and denotes another great communicative tool which can be used very effectively with our siblings. It is only by continued ego strokes that our children will listen to your message and become motivated to do more of your bidding. Enthusiasm also begins with "E"...and should be felt during your encounters with your children, because like the common cold it is very catching. Unlike the cold, its effect is positive and health-enhancing.

"N" is for the degree of Neutrality you show when handling sibling disputes. Let someone else uncover the guilty party in any quarrel if you are the judge who must mete out punishment.

Time begins with "T"...and ends when you stop giving enough of it to satisfy your children's desire to be heard on what they think is important to them. Make sure their time does not become your time, or they quit confiding in you and go elsewhere.

The "S" closes the word "Parents", and with good reason. It represents Stability, Self-Esteem, Sincerity, Self-Reliance...all qualities involved in Successful child-rearing. Once they possess these mental attributes, the world becomes their playground, so that it behooves parents to become role models and use these concepts that children will emulate, and Succeed!

# Twenty Eight

# "Show Me Yours and...

...I'll show you mine!"

Do you remember playing this game when curiosity about your sexuality first occurred?  Later, for school purposes, the game was amended to Show and Tell, with only one participant at a time.  I watch and listen to this game being played endlessly by people anywhere they can find an audience.  Complete strangers will be exchanging recipes and operations they survived (obviously) within minutes of getting into a bagel or supermarket line.  Usually it's the Express Line (12 items or less) because they have found this one to be the *slowest* in the store.  Huh?

Anyway, because I have become a fairly good listener, I find out things from strangers within two minutes after meeting them; things that their "shrinks" took three years to unearth.  I wonder at this compulsion to "confess" to a stranger things only a priest, rabbi or psycho-healer usually gets his ears on.  Perhaps this is a cheap form of therapy, a sort of catharsis to purify their ailing souls.  Whatever the reason, it leaves the listener worse off than the teller, since the burden has now been hoisted on a new set of innocent shoulders.  Unless, of course, the teller does this to relive the pain and agony...a sort of self-punitive action designed to ward off a greater punishment by a "vengeful" god.

Whatever the reasons, the end result reminds me of Max, a beautiful great dane, weighing in at over 150 pounds.  Max was owned by a client of mine.  Each time I visited his home the same scenario took place.  As my client and I sat in his living room discussing business Max would saunter in, pass wind (quietly), and leave the room at once.  No dummy he.  Those of us remaining in the room would have to find life-support systems very quickly, or succumb to Max's sneaky gas attack.

What I'm trying to say is that if these strangers want to talk to us, let it be constructive conversation.   Perhaps paying a legitimate compliment about clothing, hair styles or well-behaved children.  That should set off some good vibes and keep the conversation on a healthier level.  Having a positive experience this early in the day can only help foster more good happenings, something we can all use daily.  After a while, you may find that getting in the regular line produces better morning tidbits, since the price of things they are purchasing will always make a good opener...as we remember the "good old days" when food and things were cheaper.

What I'm suggesting is that you pick your best shot at hearing good news early in the morning, since this will help set up your day on a higher mental scale.  Maybe you have to change your bagel store...or even supermarket.  It will be well worth it.

# Twenty Nine

# Dunkin' Dogs 'n Dolphins

This is a very short story about dolphins, donuts and dogs. On my way to the Center for Successful Living yesterday, I saw a beautiful golden retriever in the car in front of mine. He moved from the back seat to the front, standing between the bucket seats. I wondered what would happen to this wonderful pet if the car had to make a very short, abrupt stop. Hitting the windshield would easily break his neck...and yet no provisions were made for the dog's safety, although he fully trusts his masters to take care of him.

This reminded me of an article I read the same week in Parade Magazine about dolphins being used to help mentally impaired, autistic and emotionally disturbed children to come out of their self-imposed, psychological shells. Another great example of the healing power...through love, that the animal kingdom manifests regularly when in contact with needy humans.

Consumers, when aroused can make things better. Recently, the large tuna canning companies stopped fishing in waters where the dolphins mix with the tuna. When are we going to have the "reverence for life" Albert Schweitzer spoke about with regards to our pets--and insist on safety features for them (seat belts?) in cars.

I was on my way to a Dunkin' Donuts place when I saw the dog in the car. While having a wholewheat donut with coffee, I idly listened to the conversation taking place there. The patrons and the waitresses were discussing all the "misses" they had in picking numbers for the lottery. No one had a winning ticket, but I heard many stories as to why they missed by a number the big payoff. I heard more "if only's" than I could shake a stick at, and once again, marveled at our unlimited ability to live in the past, or to try and change it. The philosopher George Santayana, wrote in his "The Life of Reason", that if we cannot remember the past, we are doomed to repeat it. I'm sure that when I return to the same Dunkin' Donuts, I'll see the same people telling once more how they almost won the big one.

I always suggest forgetting the past...while retaining the important lessons it taught us. I believe in using the lessons as stepping stones as we head toward a better future. A "bitter" future is what we plan for when we continue to include the negative past, as it turns into stumbling blocks.

Getting back to our pets. The lessons from my past reminded me not to treat them as we do humans, but rather as something special, because unlike most of us, they only give *unconditional* love. If that's not a lesson for us to follow, pray tell what is. I miss the cats and dogs which shared my past life because I did learn about love, patience and especially forgiveness from them all.

# *Thirty*

# Training! #*+$@

You're probably wondering why I put the "curse" signs after the word "training". Because I'm pissed, that's why. I have just perused my "fictionary" for the meaning of the word, and I don't like what I read. To boot: *Train*...to direct the growth by bending, pruning and tying; also--to form by instruction, discipline or drill. Just think. In order to "train" people we must bend, prune, tie up, instruct, discipline and drill. All this done to change our minds so that we will conform to the masses. And all this will be done on nature's greatest miracle, the human mind. That's why I cursed.

Instead of "steering" the mind...or developing our potential by appealing to our innate abilities, trainers have decided to use the same techniques Pavlov used on his experimental dogs and circus trainers use on their animals. Reward and punishment are their tools (weapons?). They still believe in forcing their ideas on others...and they use the degreed letters behind their names as fulcrum to move trainees into compliance. Reminds me of the famed philosopher Emerson, who tried to get a calf out of the path of a storm by *pushing* it from the back. Needless to say, it didn't work. Along came the milkmaid, who stuck a finger in the calf's mouth and *led* it gently into the barn. The lesson was not lost on Emerson, and he discusses its implications often in his philosophical essays.

Yesterday I worked with a local Metropolitan Life office. I was advertised as a motivational trainer to the sales reps, whom I prefer to call Problem-Solvers. For two and a half hours I did not train anyone, but offered options to them, allowing their own intelligence to guide them into making new and favorable decisions with regards to their careers. We discussed at length, the reasons why most of us work at an average of 1/50th of our full potential; then we reviewed the best ways to eliminate the negative past and plunge full steam ahead into a better, more profitable future.

As usual, I learned as much from them as they learned from me, thus "training" me to do even better the next time. But the training involved none of the manipulative techniques which came out of my Webster's lexicon. *I have an open mind*, willing to absorb new information from any source available, without prejudice against my "teacher"...whoever that may be.

Why do people continue to need training all the time? Why doesn't it take the first time? Because we are busily teaching people *how to,* and we don't spend enough training dollars on helping them *want to* use the how to. Motivation, in order to work permanently, must come from within. Trainers should help draw forth this great human quality, and nurture it when it appears.

# *Thirty One*

# Goldfish

If you have goldfish, and want to be entertained, do the following sometime. Take them out of the small round bowl which is their home, and put them in the waterfilled bathtub. Now, sit back and watch. They will go to one end of the bathtub and begin swimming in a circular motion, never larger than the size of their previous home, the bowl. You'll probably laugh at this, wondering at the naivete of the goldfish...who don't have enough sense to take advantage of their new, gigantic surroundings. Now, get up from your perch (no fish-pun intended here) and go to the bathroom mirror, look in and laugh--wondering at your naivete for not having enough sense to take advantage of *your* full potential.

I have seen figures ranging from 1/10th of 1% to 10% when experts describe the amount of human potential we use on a daily basis. The figures don't really matter; what does is the fact that we only use a fraction of our innate potential. Whether the number is 10%, as researched by William James, the father of psychology...or the more recent figure of 2% (Stanford University), it's obvious we have much room to grow. In order to do so, we have to get past the initial 15,000 plus negatives programmed into us before we were old enough to filter out junk messages. Every time we relive one of our negative messages, we are re-infecting our mind, making it easier to accept *new negative* input. The more times we accept new "baddies", it becomes easier to bring up the old ones, and thus continue the vicious cycle.

Our famous circular goldfish learned his ways from constant hits against the invisible glass. We, on the other hand, learned from constant hits against our vulnerable ego, invisibly inflicted by careless words spoken by those who love us. Most of the time they meant well, but treated us exactly as they were treated. In order to break the continuity of negativity, one must choose to stop accepting the wrong messages...and must replace them with a new philosophy based on the concept that we are made in God's image, and need never feel inferior just because others try to pin that label on us. As Eleanor Roosevelt once said: *"No one can make you feel inferior without your permission."* Deny this permission, both from the outside and your self-talk, and watch your self-esteem take on new meaning.

In the circus, elephants and fleas are trained the same way as the gold-fish. We are neither elephants nor fleas. We can choose our training based on modern, transpersonal psychology. This discipline says that we are more than singular human beings. We are part of the greater world, transcending our individual bodies as part of Universal Intelligence, and we can tap into this immeasurable power at will. I say, let's do it, starting *now!*

# Thirty Two.

# Pessimism

Pessimism is the ultimate ignorance.  I say this without reservation, since a good (bad) part of my life was spent treading water in a stagnant pool of pessimism.  I vividly remember my motto for many years: "Always expect the worst, and you'll never be disappointed."  And you know what...I was not disappointed.  For a time, I changed jobs faster than my underwear.  Each time something good was about to happen, I sabotaged it.  In those days, I might well have pasted the now "in" bumper sticker, *shit happens* to the rear of my car.  I walked around with what I called a *superior* inferiority complex, because mine was so much bigger than yours.

After it dawned on me that most of my negativity had external roots, I began to do what Socrates told us two millenia ago.  I started to "know myself".  I stopped reading novels (two per week on the average) and began using this valuable time for self help books, tapes and seminars.  Guess what?  After a time, I found that I actually enjoyed being me, and being with me.  I'm okay, you're okay began to make sense as a philosophy to live by.  I stopped being hyper-critical and judgmental, and found myself being criticized less by my peers.  As I did these things, my stress level went down, and pessimism made room for optimism.  My new credo could read: *"Always expect the best and you'll seldom be disappointed"*.

When U-Thant was Secretary General of the United Nations, he once spoke of mankind's biggest problem.  He said that people in general don't know how to experience happiness.  His remark included *billions of people!* He reminded me of the wise Lincoln, who put it this way: "People are just about as happy as they make up their minds to be!"  Thus did our great president relegate the responsibility for happiness on ourselves.

Two bums are sitting on a park bench, watching cars go by.  As a chauffeur-driven Rolls Royce appears, with a very rich looking man smoking a cigar in the back seat, one of the bums turns to the other and says: "There but for *me*...go I!"

We were given at birth all we will ever need to succeed in life.  It is up to us to rediscover the positive mental attitude we are so richly endowed with.  We must learn to transcend our self-imposed inner limits.  If pessimism is truly the height of ignorance, optimism must be the height of knowledge!

# Thirty Three

# Grrrrrrr......!

Do you GRoan your way through work...GRovel for your boss...GRind your molars...GRieve over what could have been...GRunt at your children...GRapple with life...GRimace at your bills...GRit your teeth...GRowl at dogs...etc.?

If some of these illustrations strike home, please remember that there is another word which begins with GR, yet has the power to *negate all of the above.* I'm referring to **GRATITUDE**...or, as I like to break it up, GReat attitude! Our attitude, when coming from within reminds us that we are God's GRreatest miracle, and as such we do not have to groan, grovel, grind, grieve, grunt, grapple, grimace, grit and growl at the hand life has dealt us.

I believe that a grateful attitude permits us to concentrate on the solution to the above complaints, and not their cause. The causes may remain for many years. How you approach them will determine how long they continue to carry the "problem" label. A solution-oriented person will immediately look for ways to relabel a cause and call it a "challenge" or "opportunity" for personal growth.

We are taught that we are never handed a problem by our Creator unless the seeds for its correction are already in our minds. We just need to water them by using imaginative thinking, and sprinkling new ideas on the so-called "dirty laundry". A little brainstorming, using a pen and pad will help clear away antiquated mental "dustballs".

Try these ideas for three weeks, which is the time necessary for a permanent habit change. You will then greet each new day with a smile and an eagerness to get on with it. Your gross value as a human being will grow proportionately, as positive people are worth much more in the business marketplace than negative ones. When GReed is replaced by **GRATITUDE**, more opportunities to be GRateful will come your way. For a good part of my life I woke up GRumpy, and infected those around me with the same kind of mood. One day, I decided that no one out there was going to change my thinking, and that it really is an inside job. For a while, I "faked it till I made it" my personal philosophy. Many times my morning "low" is equal to someone else's high for the day.

Those who know me stop asking how I feel, because they know my answer will be an affirmation for my day. I always reply "Fantastic...but I'll get better!" It works for me.

Find a positive affirmation that you can believe and live with; use it often and watch it become part of you psyche.

# Thirty Four

# Friendship

Friendship is the easiest quality to cultivate. The main rule is: "Talk about the other person's interests." That's it! It simply means forgetting the *I am* self, and concentrating on what the friend-to-be wants to talk about. For example; last night on my way to dinner with my wife and two friends, we ran into another couple they knew. As soon as I detected an accent when the lady spoke, I asked about her country of origin. When she said Peru I quickly asked if she had brought the Peruvian national treasure with her. I was referring to Yma Sumac, the great female singer whose amazing range reached *five octaves*. She beamed, much surprised, and proceeded to talk about Yma Sumac, preeminent singer of the late 1940s and '50s, who graced many technicolor movies with her commanding presence. After this exchange, everything went smoothly. I'm sure I'll be remembered by her as a great conversationalist, although she did most of the talking.

Rule #2 is...become a great listener! I cannot emphasize this skill too much. It separates acquaintances from friendships. People are drawn magnetically to good listeners, since they are few and far between. After all, since most spouses, bosses, co-workers and children suffer from a malady known as "listening with a deaf ear"...a true listener can acquire new friends at will.

The friendly listener understands that the tone used by others is very important, more so than the words themselves. The communication experts now tell us the ratio of tone vs. words is 5.5 times in favor of *tone*! Tone reveals the feelings behind the words. Thus, the words very often can belie the true emotion one feels. Learn to tune in to feelings, and friendships will abound. And that's Rule #3.

Finally, and still very important, is the fourth, and last rule. Listen because you really care, and because you are honestly interested in what other people think and feel. Don't fake it; I guarantee you'll be found out, and potential friendships will melt away like ice cream on a hot stove.

P.S. *Listening is loving*! I'm sure you'll agree there's far too little of that going around these days.

# Thirty Five

# Bathrooms

This week, the toilet paper in the master bathroom came dangerously close to being *pink*! My wife Janet, with whom I share this bathroom tells me it's *peach*! I can't tell you how many pink peaches I've eaten in my day. Anyway my son Joseph agrees with his mom. (After all, I'm only a stepfather). He thinks I'm outvoted, until I remind him that he (age 15) does not live in a democratic home but a dictatorship. He then retreats to *his* bedroom or *his* bathroom. At least they are *his* monthly until the mortgage is due. Then, for a day, he relinquishes all ownership to the rooms. When the mortgage payment is made, he repossesses both rooms for another 30 or 31 days. He's a good son and yet, when discussing his age recently with two ministers and their wives, all four chorused as one voice: "We will pray for you!" Fortunately for me, I only accept negatives from photo shops.

Getting back to bathrooms, I may have to use (rent?) Joseph's more often, or use the guest bathroom downstairs, which is not *truly* a bathroom, since it has no bath, not even a shower stall. Anyway, its medicine cabinet now holds toothpaste, a toothbrush, shaving cream and razor and dental floss. I am now ready for any emergency, should both upstairs bathrooms be occupied at the same time. I can live with that since the paper is white downstairs...in a totally black bathroom. Black sink, commode and walls. Makes a nice contrast with the white. But pink? Does not go well with me. Since I read a lot in the bathroom, it took me days to realize I'd been subliminally seduced into using the pink. What next? I now double check my bath towel for minute color changes. It's still beige, but I know beige is only a few shades away from pink. Et tu, Janet?

This being my final marriage, I must make allowances for individual taste. But *pink* toilet paper? I once tried sneaking in a light blue roll, but this lasted only until my wife came home. Perhaps I should just let it go, and remember that in the bathroom at least: All's well that ends well! My colorologist would probably be horrified to find out that I have blue, black, gray, maroon and white underwear; but no pink to match Janet's latest foray into the subtleties of *peach/pink*. Perhaps if I wore rose-colored glasses...oh well!

# Thirty Six

# Educare

Educare comes from the Latin, and means to draw forth from within. I'd like to suggest a new and much needed interpretation of this word, and call it edu-*care*! Meaning that whether we draw forth what is already there, or *instruct*...teach from the outside *structured* information, we should put more care into the lessons. I refer to both the home and the school, since both become very important in the early training years.

The less we Instruct (a left-brain function) and the more we draw forth from within (a right-brain function) through Insight, Intuition and Inspiration, the better the student will learn to handle life's constant challenges. Dealing on a daily basis with introverts, extroverts, ambiverts and now, perverts, can be made easier if we concentrate on *people skills* rather than career skills when children are still very young. Stanford University Human Resources Division made a study of successful careers. It came up with the following data. Success is 87 1/2% *people skills*, and 12 1/2% Job Skills. Please don't misunderstand; although job skills are worth only 12 1/2%, you must *know* your job 100%.

I suggest continuing training of our teachers, as well as parents on the use of people skills. P.Q.s (Personality Quotient) have traditionally out-earned I.Q.s (Intelligence Quotient). One study on the subject showed that the P.Q.s earned over three times as much as the I.Q.s from the same graduating classes in just 10 years.

As for parents, we can never learn enough about people-handling. We deal not only with our children daily, but also business associates, relatives, peers and others with whom proper communication is crucial. When the preeminent psychologist Leo Buscaglia mailed out 1,000 questionnaires to couples married for many years, fully 85% of the 600+ who responded, listed **COMMUNICATION** as the number one need. Communication *means* people skills. 'Nuff said!

# Thirty Seven

# Value-Added

Now that most of us have already earned our Ph.D. in Pain and Despair where life is concerned, it is time to retrench our thoughts and feelings, and enter a new phase of life. For as the great philosopher George Santayana pointed out: "Those who cannot remember the past are condemned to repeat it!" We strongly recommend using the past as a springboard into the future, without dwelling on past errors, yet knowing we made them. For example, if we can just turn our human relations with others into *humane relations*...with the extra E standing for Empathy, Encouragement, Enthusiasm and Excellence when dealing with our peers, friends, relatives and even strangers...we would find that our personal pain and despair would decrease proportionately. In business, there is a term known as Value-Added. This means we give something extra, above and beyond the product or service to the client in order to facilitate the transaction.

I believe value-added must be used with people, not just products. Using the above-mentioned four E's as a starter, we can multiply our effectiveness when dealing with others.

This means we have to stop listening to the wrong B.S. No, not the B.S. we are all familiar with; I mean the wrong Belief System. If the research done by Stanford University in the '80s is correct, the average person today uses only about 2% of his or her potential. This means we can grow geometrically in accomplishment while adding only 1% more usability of our skills...since 1% means an increase of 50% of the current 2% we are now using. My concern is that when we leave this earth, ST. Peter will not ask how we used our 2% in our lives. He will want to know why we wasted 98% of what his Boss (and ours) gave us at birth. *Are you ready with an answer to that question?*

I believe we grow into maturity by extending ourselves through others. All of the "great" men and women of history are known for what they did for *others*, not the self(ish). In Value-Added diplomacy, I feel that the more we give of ourselves, the more we will remain with. After all, nature does abhor a vacuum. One of my mentors, Johann Wolfgang Von Goethe wrote what I believe epitomizes Humane Relations best: "If we take people as they are, we make them worse. If we treat them as if they were what they ought to be, we help them to become what they are capable of being!" He obviously looked beyond the 2% people were showing, and addressed the untapped 98%, thus helping to release it.

# Thirty Eight

# Bumper Stickers

Being a voracious reader, my eyes will latch on to anything that has words on it. Hence, my love for bumper stickers, plus vanity license plates (mine reads MOTIVATR), and what's written on the license frames.

This past week, I concentrated on the "I (heart) such and such or so and so". I'll use the word love for the proverbial red heart on the stickers.

-I love my dog.

-I love my cat.

-I love my ferret.

-I love my parrot, doberman, schnauzer, German Shepherd, etc...

What I have not yet seen is one that says:

-I love my wife!

-I love my husband!

-I love my mother!

-I love my father!...or my children, parents, in-laws, etc.....

Why do we advertise our love for non-human life only? Are we ashamed to admit love for anyone except a pet?

Well, I'm not ashamed! I love my wife and I love my son! What do you suppose would happen if you stopped reading this vignette, went over to your spouse or child...and just said: "Just thought I'd drop by and tell you I love you!" After he/she got up from the floor, he/she'd want to know what you did wrong ...and felt guilty about. Or, they might think that you lost your marbles. After all, in today's society we usually speak of love after we just lost someone, when they can't hear it anymore. What an absolute waste of time and emotion. The time to tell people you love them is now, and the heck with what's "proper" and acceptable in today's society.

Who then will be the first to print bumper stickers that say: "I love my...(family member)? I'll be your first customer, and hopefully not your last and only one.

Parents, tell your kids you love them...even if you feel like strangling them at times. Read the obituaries for a few days and see how soon we may be parted from our loved one.s

Children, tell your parents you love them. Now, while they are still alive, and a pain in your young butt sometimes. Tell your brothers and sisters you love them. You don't have to like everything your family does, but you should love them in spite of their idiosyncrasies. After all, who ever said that you were perfect?

# Thirty Nine

## 56 Shoes

When we moved from a condo to our own home two years ago, I brought my labeled boxes into our new bedroom for unpacking. This room contains a large walk-in closet...a new luxury for my wife and I. We decided to share the closet evenly, left side for me and right side for my wife. As I unpacked my shoes, I noticed that my half filled up very quickly. I looked around. My wife was away for the day, so I continued to fill the full floor (inverted U-shape) with my shoes only. Checked my boxes again and found more of my shoes. Dismayed at this point, I counted my collection. Twenty-eight pairs of shoes...and I was not even married to Mrs. Marcos (3,000 pairs).

Being somewhat of an analytical, I decided to try and uncover the reason why I needed enough shoes to guarantee I would not have to wear a pair more than once in February of each year. The answer came quickly. In Belgium, my brother and I wore second hand shoes sent to us from America by our grandparents. In Casablanca, Morocco, we wore rubber cutouts from used tires, with a leather strap attached to them.

Once in the United States, my father never owned more than two pairs of shoes. One pair for work, and one for social and religious occasions.

I subconsciously decided never to be in lack of shoes again. This meant I was dragging my *negative past* into the present, and letting it control my current needs. Once I saw the problem, I proceeded to use up as many pairs as possible without replacing them. I am now at half-point, with only 14 pairs left. My goal is to reach six, three for lectures/seminars and three for pleasure. As one wise wit once said: "Don't look back (into the past) unless you want to go back!" Metaphorically speaking, it's as if you were driving on a busy highway at 75 miles per hour, looking into the rearview mirror much of the time. *Very dangerous!*

I believe I may have had the same problem with food. Having been deprived of normal portions for three years as a refugee, I now carry an extra 12 pounds for "protection" (insulation?). Or is it just because I love good food and it is so readily available in all parts of the United States? Only my subconscious knows for sure, and it isn't ready to tell. I can tell you one thing for sure, the saying "You are what you eat" is all wrong. The truth is, "*You eat what you are!*" Using poetic license, I can also put it this way..."as you think of yourself deep in your heart, so you will eat!"

P.S. No, my shoes did not stay for long on my wife's side of the closet. They came "flying out" the moment she set eyes on my fancy footwork.

# *Forty*

# Forgiveness

I'm not necessarily against lengthy, conventional and expensive therapy. I'm not really for it either. I have friends in the mental health field, as well as friends who see those in the mental health field. As a result of observing both sides, I've come to some personal conclusions.

My first thought comes from my knowledge of motivation. If it is indeed true that a person is the result of what he/she thinks about often, what then is the purpose of digging up the negative past, complete with its traumas and emotional distress? It is a proven fact that what we repeat we *reinforce*. Ivan Pavlov became world famous working on the science of conditioning.

Much neurosis comes from anger, fear, jealousy, resentment, envy and hatred...at both the *self* and *others*. With many of us these have become habit-forming, self-destructive feelings. Transpersonal psychology goes beyond the individual, and helps us live in the now, not in the painful past. The question becomes, "How can we quickly develop a *now attitude*, and begin to look into a brighter future"?

I have found the 21-day Forgiveness Diet works well on those who are truly ready to change and improve their lives. It calls for making up a full list of all the people (*especially* family) who we believe have hurt us in any way whatsoever. Then, for three weeks, we look at each name daily and in normal voice, forgive them. It only works when we both *think* and *feel* the words as they are spoken. At the bottom of the list is our own name; it too must be addressed daily. By forgiving and accepting people as they *are*, and not as we would like them to *be*...we begin the process of self-healing, without digging into the past for negative input. Forgiveness is a Positive Act, which frees us from the chains that bind us to all past tormentors. We can then resume our relationship in full control of our feelings, not at the mercy of others.

Remember that to forgive is to give up resentment. A low self-esteem is really self-resentment manifesting in our life. Who in his right mind needs this?

# *Forty One*

# Suicide

"Suicide Book a Lively Seller" screams the Newsday headline. The latest "how-to" has become #1 on the New York Time hardcover best-seller list. I have a real problem with this latest foray into the non-fiction section of your bookstore. I worry over terms such as "unbearable suffering", which can be purely psychological and emotional pain. Is this then an O.K. for suicide even though there is no physical trauma attached to the decision? Also, can this not be used by people just wanting to get rid of unwanted relatives? Seems to be a "carte blanche" for suicide-prone persons who needed "permission" to do the deed.

Some of the chapters include the illuminating "How Do You Get the Magic Pills?", and for couples the vacation-like "Going Together?" It seems to me highly improbable that a couple would need the "Self-Deliverance Via the Plastic Bag" (another chapter heading for the "sanitary" types) at exactly the same time. This means that at least one of them has taken his/her life too soon.

Right now over 100,000 copies are out; this means any depressed person, including teenagers or older, can find out for only $20 how to escape into the world of non-existence.

It's a sad commentary on our society that this book could get such publicity, while the real heroes of life are so often neglected by those who need them the most. I'm talking about authors such as Wayne Dyer, Louise Hay, Bernie Siegel, et. al....whose works help people to reduce , and in many cases eliminate pain, both physical and mental. I also include holistic health practitioners, the New Thought ministers, chiropractors...and all those who concentrate on making and keeping people well! There are enough books, tapes, seminars and lectures for those who want to save their lives.

All I know is that if I find out that my wife is asking around about those *"magic pills"* I am going to run as fast as I can, as far as I can. As it is, I have already joined millions of American who are into a slow-suicide mode...eating chemical-infested foods and drinks. I just don't want to rush into anything I can't get out of! Suicide is so *permanent*!

# Forty Two.

# A Timely Fairy Tale

This story is about an antique clock and a new digital calculator/clock. One day the calculator/clock was placed next to the antique clock, and, true to its young age, began to babble at breakneck speed. The older and much wiser clock, urged it to slow down or it would never see the next century. Here is some of their dialogue:

C/C: How old are you?

A: I'm not sure...I lost count after the first hundred years.

C/C: How fast does your clock beat?

A: Twice per second.

C/C: Wow! That means that you beat...let's see...click/click...you beat 120 times per minute.

A: I guess so. I never tried to figure it out.

C/C: It's real easy for me because of my built-in calculator. If you beat 120 times per minute, you must beat...hmm...click/click....7,800 times per hour. Boy, that sure is a lot of beats.

A: You really think so?

C/C: Do I ever! Let's continue and figure this out...7,800 times, 24 hours per day, click/click...and you have 172,800 per day! Wow!

A: Hmmm. That does sound like a lot of beats.

C/C: You know, my calculator part is hardly warmed up. Let's take this further and see where it leads. We take the 172,800 and multiply by 365 days...and we got...Holy Cow!....63,000,000 per year!

A: Those certainly are big numbers.

C/C: Heck, you ain't seen nothin' yet. You say you're at least 100 years old. If we multiply your 63 million by 100, you'll get...click/click...I can't do it; the numbers are running off my screen.

A: Slow down, kid. This one's easy, even for me. Just add two zeros to the 63,000,000 and you get 6,300,000,000...6.3 billion.

At that, the calculator/clock fainted. Soon after, when he revived, he continued his conversation with the antique clock,

C/C: I can't believe what you just said to me. You admitted that over the past century you beat over 6.3 billion times. How is it possible for you to do that without having a nervous breakdown at some point?

A: Well, you see, I never looked at it the way you did. Never added up the total times my pendulum swung. I only *concentrated on the next beat*...thinking only of the next beat made it easy!

Question. Are you concentrating on the next few minutes of your life, or worried because you are looking too far ahead?

# Forty Three

# Positive Selling

Selling yourself and your ideas to others is one of your most important needs. How would you like to learn the secret of selling yourself and your ideas so that more people will want to do as you suggest? Here are some basic rules to help you.

The first rule: Learn to deal with people on an emotional level. Numerous studies have shown that our buying habits follow a ninety to ten formula. In other words, our thinking brain is only 10% as large as our feeling brain. Research continually points to the fact that success in any endeavor is determined by attitudes in life rather than by aptitudes--on a ratio of six to one. Speaking to people using factual information will not move them toward acceptance of your ideas. To move people, you must motivate by stirring emotions. Many of us are literally short sighted when it comes to other people. As a result, the way we see them is the way we end up treating them. As we end up treating them, they end up becoming. You have the power to change people by the way you see and treat them.

Several years ago, a survey of 100 self-made millionaires showed only one common denominator that bound them together. These highly successful men and women could only see the good in people. They were people builders, rather than critics. Critics leave their victims worse off for having met them. As for "constructive criticism", there is no such thing. The words belie the term. A critic could never understand what Harvey Firestone once said, "You get the best out of others when you give the best of yourself."

Here's rule number 2: Do not do to others what you would not want done to you. Look at the world through their eyes, not your eyes. Say and do what will excite and interest them. Make them feel important. You can change lives by using these age-old concepts, and they cost you nothing. Human relations do not work, humane relations do. The difference in the word is an "E"--perhaps standing for Extra Effort. You can acquire a Ph.D. (People handling Doctorate) overnight once you begin to use this non-magical formula.

Finally, here's rule number three: Cultivate the art of being dependable. People will pay you more both in money and attention, when you exhibit "depend-ability" over and above ability. While ability in this world is common, depend-ability is rare. So, become the rare person you were meant to be; one who is a people builder, who practices humane relations. Also, let people know they can depend on you.

# Forty Four

# Unconditional Love

The Chinese language has no alphabet. Therefore, when written, it is most intriguing. The Chinese draw symbols that mean entire words, rather than using individual letters in combination to create different words. Some of the symbols used bespeak the profound wisdom to be found in the ancient Chinese philosophy.

For example, when you combine the Chinese word symbols for "man" and "woman", you get the symbol for "good". It certainly can be for everyone, if we would only learn to treat our mates with unconditional love. Doing that properly helps bring out the hidden splendor which is everyone's natural inheritance at birth. The problem is, we attach too many conditions to our love.

Many of us spend most of our lives doling out love on an "if" basis. You'll notice that the word "if" is the middle half of the word "life". You'll also recall that the New Testament says, "Love they neighbor as thyself." It doesn't say, "Love thy neighbor if'." In fact, we do love, dislike or hate our neighbor in the same proportion that we love, dislike or hate ourselves. We do this by projecting to the outside world our own healthy or poor self image...thereby fulfilling the prophecy of "love". Poor self image is usually a result of lack of love.

To be loved means to be important to someone...and feeling important is as important to human beings as breathing. When was the last time someone made you feel important? When did you last make someone feel important? When I teach selling skills, I stress the fact that people will buy almost anything if they are made to feel important in the process.

Feeling important also brings respect. Rodney Dangerfield has made a fortune parroting our main complaint, "I don't get no respect—no respect at all!" Respect from others comes only after your own self respect emerges. Self respect comes easily when someone loves you. That someone should first be you. I'm not talking about narcissistic, self love. I mean the kind you have for yourself because you are a good person and helping others gives you great satisfaction. Then you can eliminate everyone else's "if" clause because you're secure in your feelings about yourself.

Systematic, in-depth soul searching will reveal to you that most of your present thoughts come from the outside world. Instead, develop and use your own intuition, or learning from within.

# Forty Five

# Non-Conformists

It is perhaps the most misunderstood quote ever uttered by a world-class American philosopher. I'm referring to the great iconoclast, Henry David Thoreau, who is revered in Europe, yet virtually ignored in the United States. His quote? The famous drummer, which goes: "If a man does not keep pace with his companions, perhaps it is because he hears a different drummer. Let him step to the music which *he* hears, however measured or far away." I accented the "he" because each of us hears music in a much different way, and *individual* tastes decide how we will react to it.

Thoreau wanted us to follow our inner sound, and not be led by the nose into the world of conformity. Something which always managed to get me into some kind of trouble in my younger years. As a confirmed non-conformist, I let my "gut" feelings guide me through the myriad trials and tribulations of my life. I wore a beard as a youth (Van Dyke) which cost me a job because I was ahead of my time. I lost a chance at a promotion because I did not want to wear the proverbial necktie to the office. I was the top producer for a very large, international sales company at the time, but conformity mattered more to management. It was a way to control the sales staff, and I have always objected to being controlled, rather than guided. I left the company with all my awards, went to another and continued to receive more sales awards for high productivity, and this *without a necktie.*

When I was much younger, my mother called me the rebel of the family, and my father said I was a revolutionist. Mom often said I'd end up in the electric chair. Actually she was right, as I did purchase an electric Barcalounger when I moved into a new apartment in New York City. All I can say is...thank God they did not knock this "craziness" out of my head, or else I would have lived a mediocre, average life. I don't believe we were meant to live like sheep. We were given the power to *think for ourselves,* yet we allow others (parents, teachers, media, authorities) to think for us, and dictate what will make us *happy*!

What makes Jacques happy has *nothing* to do with what makes you happy. Hopefully we can both be happy without stepping on each others' needs. If we find that the same things make us happy, so much the better. It's a bonus handed down to us by life, and we should develop an attitude of gratitude for life's gifts.

By the way, have you noticed how many so-called non-conformists *conform to each other*! Just watch kids in their peer groups...same labels, hairdos, etc...Adults are the same...monkey see, monkey do... which is a lot of doo-doo!

# Forty Six

# E.S.P.

My subject deals with the wrong type of ESP, the kind which destroys many lives daily. This one stands for Exaggerated Self-Pity, not Extra-Sensory Perception. I see the results of it everywhere, and hear about it more times than I care to. It always begins with the ever-present "I", followed by the "my", "me", "mine", "to me", etc. The ESP personality defines life in terms of "my ulcers", "my son-in-law", "my problems". It wallows in self-pity, muttering "poor l'il ol' me" and "nobody loves me", until the words fulfill their self prophecy, at which point the person does become a *victim of life.*

Once we call an ulcer "my ulcer", we take possession of it forever. When we attach the personal pronoun to a problem, using mental crazy glue, we then own the illness, bad happening or accident. As a victim, we can safely retreat into our self-pity, thus reinforcing it.

There is a way out of this self inflicted trap. We must go back to basics, and truly understand what Extra-Sensory Perception really means.

This is the perception above and beyond the senses, or left brain, which is used primarily to insure our survival. The perception I refer to is the original input we inherited at birth, our direct connection to our Creator. This includes the innate, insight, intuition, inspiration and imagination. If we are what we have been taught...made in God's image, then imagination is God in action.

This means that by shifting our mental emphasis from left brain to right where this perception lives, we can change our way of thinking. When we change our thinking, we change our lives. Instead of wallowing in self-pity, a *whiner* can become a *winner!* Winners possess courage, kindness, wonder, energy and love. Whiners are possessed by rage, fury, terror, fear and hate. I have worn both sets of feelings in my once tumultuous life; I chose to become a winner.

Choosing means exactly that. We can choose the thoughts we want to identify with, and thus eliminate through non-use the old messages of inferiority. Then our new self-image can match our creator's, and we can forget self-pity and its twin brother...a low self-esteem. Change the negative affirmations. Use positive ones instead, and miracle will follow miracle, as life truly becomes worthwhile living!

Change the letter "H" (self-Hate) to "N" (self-Nurture) and you have changed wHiner to wiNner!

# Forty Seven

# Selling Yourself

Selling yourself and your ideas to friends, clients, peers or even family, takes skill. If they are to buy what you say you must become a diplomat without portfolio. I believe the octet I made up for my sales training seminars will help you to better understand one-on-one communications:

**Show and Tell...**

**Fail to Sell!**

**If You Talk...**

**They Will Balk!**

**So Instead...**

**Use Your Head!**

**Ask Them 'Y"?...**

**And They'll Buy!**

The reason this works best is because people usually listen far more carefully when you are discussing their favorite subject: Them! By asking questions, rather than making statements, you are getting them to become more fully involved in the communicative process. Psychological studies have shown that most of us are in the I-me-mine mode 93% of our awake time. Therefore, it stands to reason that when we appeal to this unholy (unhealthy?) trio, we will have their full attention.

It works very well when selling a product or service. I always recommend beginning the interview with an in-depth questionnaire, thus getting to the root of the prospect's problem. You can find out more about anyone just asking six pointed questions than you can conversing with them for two hours.

During my motivational therapy sessions, my clients tell me within *minutes* some of their best-kept secrets. Why? Because my questions show *I truly care for them!* This attitude will open more chances for friendships and business than the "professional" approach most sales manuals recommend. I'd rather come across as a truly caring amateur than a cold, calculating professional. This has worked for me in the past when I won several International Awards in selling, while competing with over 14,000 sales "professionals". Job skills we know account for only 12 1/2% of sales success. *People skills* account for the rest. People skills must be used with integrity; body language will betray the lack of this most important quality when communicating with others. As Ralph Waldo Emerson once wrote: "What you are screams *so loud* I can't hear what you *say!*"

If you want people to become interested in you, and buy (you) or from you, first become interested in them. Then watch friendships, as well as sales bloom.

# Forty Eight

# The Ten Forgetments

Since our self-talk (intalk) is based on worry 77% of the time, (according to the new research) I'd like to submit a set of *10 negative affirmations*...which I strongly recommend we erase from our daily vocabulary. They all include strong action words, which make them difficult to surrender.

Here is my list:

1 - court danger...2 - invite disaster...3 - entertain doubt...4 - expect the worst...5 - accept our fate...6 - hold a grudge...7 - wallow in pity...8 - drown in sorrow...9 - kill with kindness...and finally, 10 - surrender to the inevitable.

A good way to give up on these bad-mouthings is to understand more about worry. Psychologists have taken worry apart to see what makes it tick. They uncovered startling facts about it. They all suggest we stop worrying because...

40% of worries *never* happen...

30% of worries are already *past*...

12% is needless, and involves worrying over our *health*...

10% is merely *petty stuff*, not worth the time spent on it...

...and *only* 8% is real, of which half (4%) is *solvable*!

This means that fully 24 out of 25 worries are absolutely *wasted time and emotion.*

Think what would happen if you stopped this mental assault on your nervous system, and turned 96% of your *worrying* time into productive channels? What a wonderful life you would then live. Of all the bipeds and quadrupeds only humans have eyes that look straight ahead. Why then do we bother to look backwards into our past, over which we no longer have dominion. We were meant to look forward, towards our future, and to think that way as well.

It's been said that people who always speak of the past, don't live long. Those who speak of the present, live average lives. Finally, those who speak of a bright future live longer than average.

Try a little test on yourself. Count the number of times you use one or more of the above *10 forgetments* in a week. Then, do as the computers do when in error...push your mental cancel button and reaffirm a positive solution at once. You'll find soon enough that you'll forget the old worries and concentrate on what's good for you and your future.

# Forty Nine

# Repetition Reinforces Recognition

Since I began my one-a-day vignettes on July 15th, there are several themes I keep repeating over and over again in my stories. The three R's of learning stand for Repetition Reinforces Recognition. Since I give my imagination free reign when writing, I have little control over what will appear on the typed page. Whatever needs repeating for emphasis gets repeated.

The more times a subject appears as part of a new vignette, the more need there must be on my part to reinforce that idea. I'll continue and trust my intuitive flashes for guidance on choosing my subject matter. The topics which seem to recur consistently include those that represent the noblest ideals, a fact that does not come as a surprise to me. The following baker's dozen headings will prove my point:

1 - Personal development...2 - self knowledge...3 - work ethic...4 - love (for self as well as others)...5 - belief system...6 - continued education...7 - goals and purpose...8 - health (mental and physical)...9 - family ties...10 - skills...11 - life changes...12 - forget past...13 - plan successful, happy future.

If you also eliminate superstition from your mental arsenal, you'll be able to recognize and accept these 13 major "trauma centers" as needing constant reform. "Don't look back, unless you want to *go back* (past)" is still excellent advice. Implementing it is simple...yet very difficult. Simple because all you have to do to change and improve is replace the *old you* with the *new you*. Difficult because we often will literally fight to the *death* to hang on to our old neuroses.

My personal plan of action to change took two methods. The first one was to stop wasting time on trash-reading, i.e., novels and *bad news*. Instead, I filled my current library with hundreds of books on personal development. My second tool for retraining and controlling my mind is the cassette player. Once again, I invested in myself by purchasing hundreds of cassettes, which tell me daily what I want to hear. I use them in my car and when I do my daily walk around the hills I live near. The trick is to back *replace* negative ideas with new Positive ones. Or rather, go back one final time and exorcise the "stinkin' thinkin'" permanently. Forgive and Forget the past...cling only to happy memories. This will do more for your self-respect and self-image than constantly dredging up the past and feeling sorry for yourself, which is self-punitive, and leads to most illnesses known today. Once you believe you're worthy you'll begin to improve your life forever.

# Fifty

# Altus

Altus, the mythical Greek bird, which flew higher and deeper than all others. It's my logo on the recently released tapes I made, which are sold at my lectures and seminars. It symbolizes my philosophy well; higher for the *external* world we live in, and deeper for what's *inside* of us...waiting to be released. I believe altus means we should be the best we can, both to the outside world, as well as the world within.

On my tapes is a saying I paraphrased: "you cannot change the wind...but you can alter your wings!" Meaning of course that although we cannot control external events, we can *always* control our *reaction* to them. But this requires a process called thinking. And there's the rub.

The FUTURIST magazine published new data recording how we Americans spend our *spare time*. Out of a total of over 40 hours per week of leisure time we now possess, exactly one hour is spent on thinking/relaxing! Between 15 and 20 hours are uselessly wasted on T.V...in order to "entertain" us, and keep us from having to think. Since thinking is the major difference between humans and the animal kingdom, and we are doing less of it each decade surveyed...are we then reverting back to our old animal status? Perhaps this explains the multiplicity of crimes, and their increased severity and brutality. We all know that the less we think, the quicker our old brain reacts in Cro-magnon fashion. Just look at the plethora of violent movies now shown in theaters and on T.V. Each new episode tries to *out-brutalize* the last one released. The result is that we are building a new mentality based on pain and torture...and this after over six millenia of organized religion.

If it still holds true that we become what we think about...and we are not doing much thinking, we must then become a product of whatever is coming in to us from external stimuli. The great humanitarian, Nobel Prize winner Dr. Albert Schweitzer was asked 50 years ago by reporters: "Dr. Schweitzer, what's wrong with people today?" He replied: "People just don't think!"..And this answer before the advent of T.V., America' s greatest time killer.

Perhaps we should rephrase the old tried and true "an apple a day keeps the doctor away" to read, "a thinking hour a day keeps the mental cobwebs away!" I place full responsibility for this change in the hands of parents and teachers, where it all begins. They can try *asking* instead of telling when communicating with the younger generation. Telling generally affects the left brain only; asking makes both brains work in tandem and results in *thinking!*

# *Fifty One*

# Wishbone or Backbone

Wishbone people go through life traveling on flights of fancy, allowing things to happen to them. They are commonly known as victims of circumstances. Diametrically opposed to them are the "backbone" individuals, those who make things happen and become the victors in life's race. They are considered to be *self-made* successes...while the "dreamers" (wishboners) can be regarded as self-made *failures*! The difference in many cases lies in their early conditioning and how they reacted when confronted with problems or adversity.

I have a very difficult time remembering my early childhood,. But if it's true that the apple does not fall far from the tree, I can certainly hypothesize. Although I lived with my family in Brussels, in a two-room apartment (kitchen and bedroom), somehow the four of us managed to live in peace and harmony. Unlike my teenage son who has his own room and bathroom...my brother and I did not have a radio, color T.V., stereo, CDs and a bicycle, as well as a closet full of clothes. But we did have a rich legacy of close family ties. Our parents did not "raise" us (we raise cabbages); instead, they nurtured us. Although poor, I never felt it until we ran because of the war, leaving our few belongings behind. By then my "backbone" had been formed. I knew life would involve a series of ups and downs, until it finally leveled off and would run a smooth course.

The world may have seen us as victims when we ran from the Nazis, and yet the war enabled us to come to the United States earlier than my parents had planned for us. I remember the simple philosophy they were brought up with in Czechoslovakia. Its tenets included mundane concepts such as honesty, integrity, work ethic, respect for elders, etc...ideas which for the most part, have become outdated in this once-great country.

Parents, for many reasons, no longer seem to have the time needed to spend with their offspring. I am stating a fact, with no judgment attached. Children may not be mature enough to understand the pressures parents undergo; therefore they judge, and become *victims* of their own inadequacies. Oscar Wilde wrote over a century ago: "Children begin by loving their parents. After a time, they judge them. Rarely, if ever, do they forgive them".

One hundred years later, psychologists understand the need for children to truly forgive their parents. Their faults notwithstanding, the truth must come out. Parents are always doing their *best*, based on their own feelings as Victims or Victors. We can change our self-image as victims, and we can become winners...by finally understanding and accepting our parents as they are, and not necessarily as we would like them to be.

# Fifty Two.

# Bias

"Once upon a time, a man whose ax was missing, suspected his neighbor's son. The boy *walked* like a thief, *looked* like a thief and *spoke* like a thief.

But the man found his ax while he was digging in the valley, and the next time he saw his neighbor's son, the boy *walked, looked and spoke* like any other child."

-Lao-tzu

Bias means prejudiced outlook. If you're never guilty of this, you may skip this vignette. Since you've chosen to continue reading, I must assume that you also have been smitten by this highly unjust malady, which seems to be passed on almost genetically from parent to child. Actually, one catches it from another person who is already infected. It is a very young child's disease, striking well before age three. To quote the popular author of "The First Three Years of Life"...Dr. Burton White: "I now believe that not more than one child in ten gets off to as good a start as he could!" This means that the odds are 9:1 against growing up unbiased.

Too often we treat people of a certain race, color or religion as if they were all alike, cloned from the same queen bee. Be they introvert, extravert, ambivert or even pervert, we still see them through "a glass darkly"...our own preconditioned ideas.

If instead we thought what if we were wrong...and not automatically act as if they were all replicated from our original "role model" of the species, peace on earth might well prevail. Many of us believe the world is too far gone to change and save. Their philosophy then becomes "Looking Out for #1"...and to hell with the rest. This C.Y.A. (Cover Your Ass) attitude is the precursor to much personal mental stress and anguish.

We all know that sheep will follow each other over a fence...even after the fence is removed. We are not sheep, and need not salivate Pavlovian-style whenever we have to make a decision on a new person. We can give people the benefit of the doubt, and treat each one on an individual basis...and not as part of our previous group-think.

If Reader's Digest, with its 31 million readers per month, is correct when it states that our prime interest is in our health, it behooves us to learn more about Wellness...and less about Illness.

Bias as an acronym (Brings In Assorted Sicknesses), is great for those on a self-destruct mission.

# Fifty Three

# Plague

There is a plague threatening the very fabric of America, and we can't seem to staunch it at this time. I call it the C.C.S., or the Chronic Complainer Syndrome. As we already know from human resources research, humans have a great need to feel important. In light of this information, it becomes understandable why we speak about ourselves up to 95% of the time in daily conversation with our peers. In order to feel (not necessarily be) important, we begin by telling others of our accomplishments, looking for approbation. When this ceases, as we run out of good things to brag about, we begin to *complain!*

Fully four out of every five words will come out in the form of a complaint, whether against someone, something or ourself! The main problem as I see it is that complainers usually are looking for a cheap *dumping ground* for their bad luck, illnesses, etc...

They don't want ad-vice (no pun intended). They want pity, compassion, sympathy, a constant listening ear.

One way out of this dilemma for the tired and bored listener, is to visualize a *plague* sign on your victim's chest. As he/she approaches and you see the sign...*duck!* If you can't duck, you must learn to use defensive tactics. You can begin to speak about your problems at length, thus turning the tables on your victim and letting him think that you have the C.C.S. You can remember a previous appointment, and make for it at once, or else you can wear your own sign on your chest saying: *"I'm a doormat...please step on me at will!"*

If regular food is the the body, then talk is food for the brain. Just as you can receive small doses of poison in your daily food intake, so can you absorb mental poison from negative talk in small, repeated doses. Enough brain poison will turn even the staunchest positive thinker into a negative shell of his/her former self.

I listen to friends and peers and relatives when they complain, but *only once.* I offer options...not ad-vice at that time, and never expect the subject to come up again as a complaint. If this doesn't work, they receive my subliminal *plague* sign, which they wear whenever I see them. I don't believe I've lost a single true friend this way. Emotional leeches, yes.

Once again I turn to the wise Chinese proverbs. This one deals with the complainer and advises the following: *"Person who says it can't be done should not interfere with person who is doing it!"*

# *Fifty Four*

# Are Goals Enough?

The cast of characters includes the following eight men and their final accomplishments in life:

One died bankrupt...one was a penniless fugitive from the law...one was insane...one served time in Sing Sing...one in another jail...and the final three were suicides.

These eight men held a meeting in one of Chicago's most prestigious hotels 25 years earlier, in 1929. At that time, five of them were presidents of:

a - the largest steel company in the United States.

b - the largest utility company in the United States.

c - the largest gas utility in the United States.

d - the New York Stock Exchange...and

e - the Bank for International Settlements.

The last three included a member of the United States Cabinet...the greatest speculator on Wall Street, and the Chairman of the world's greatest monopoly.

It's quite safe to assume that these eight powerful men reached their goals in life, since they all climbed to the top of their chosen professions. I can easily guarantee that their fall was much quicker than their rise. The reasons? Probably the same for all of them, although in varying degrees.

As they became wealthier, they replaced their original values for more power. Spouses and children were left behind in the proverbial dust, and their love for people was transferred to things. As their values changed, so did their lives. The individual falls they experienced were precipitated in part by an all-consuming greed for more.

I hope the lesson is not missed. What happened in 1929 to eight very prominent businessmen can happen today if the conditions are the same. We cannot expect a good family life if we put careers at the top of our priorities. I believe any goals we set should be arrived at by mutual consent. More importantly, achievers have a purpose above and beyond mere financial goals. They are not the takers of the world; they believe in giving back part of what they manage to amass...thus keeping the economy moving.

Havelock Ellis (1859-1939) wrote in "The Dance of Life": "...it is not the attainment of the goal that matters, it is the things that are met with by the way." The trick here is to make your goals subservient to a greater purpose. Then the journey in life will keep you happier than the end result ever could. Goals are great in soccer, but I really believe the game should be the main reason for engaging in that sport. Had my *purpose* been clearer than my goals, I would have been spared much frustration in my early career days.

# Fifty Five
# Job or Vacation

Concluding a 16 year study of over 350,000 job applicants, the California State University (at Fullerton) reported that 80% were in the *wrong jobs!* A second study done by the Marketing Survey and Research Corporation confirmed the fact that fully four out of five employees in America are not doing what they are best suited for in the workplace. Small wonder that the 80/20 ratio first formulated by Vilfredo Pareto in 1896, still haunts us. This is the famous calculation done with regards to the "unequal distribution of wealth", as he called it. It means that 20% of the work force accomplishes 80% of the results, thereby earning 4/5th's of the money circulated via salaries, commissions, bonuses, etc...Since anger and frustration generally follow when one is unhappy on the job, it becomes easy to understand why sickness and absenteeism are rampant within the business community.

In contrast to this stark picture of workers in the United States, I just finished reading a truly heartwarming story in Parade Magazine. It deals with Dr. Matthew Warpick, who just celebrated his 90th birthday at his *office*, where he continues his medical practice, six days a week. There's a man who knew what he wanted from the first day he opened his office in 1926. He could easily have joined the top 5% in earnings in the medical profession. Instead, he chose to remain in what is now a crime ridden neighborhood. I believe he and Dr. Albert Schweitzer would have become great friends had they met, since they both exemplify the highest humanitarian standards.

Talk about ethical philosophers; both men espoused the idea of altruistic egoism, wherein they give of themselves for the sole pleasure of feeling good. To quote Dr. Warpick: "The reward in this type of practice is knowing that you're helping people, people who need you. That keeps you alive." Another quote from the doctor: "The people who live in this area are responsible for me being able to live this long. They tell me, 'Doctor, don't retire. We need you.'"

Twenty-five years ago, Dr. Warpick (then age 65) lost his admitting privileges at major New York hospitals. I believe this to be *their loss*. It's one thing to forcefully retire an unhappy worker, but to deprive the world of gifted men...this is heresy.

Someone once said: "Love your work, and work your love." I firmly believe there would be more 90-year old productive members of society if we believed in and followed this wise council. My suggestion for you is simple: Stand back and analyze what you are now doing to earn your daily bread. Do you feel really good about the work...or is there some inner yearning for other work? If there is, find it...*do it*, and enjoy life more fully!

# 55 M.P.H.or Bust

You're driving your new car on the expressway, and you stop every few miles when you see the 55 MPH sign. You get out of your car, replace the sign with your own, which reads 1.1 MPH, then proceed (at 1.1 MPH) until the next one, etc...If you think this sounds ridiculous, consider the following. At birth, we are all given an innate *success mechanism*...a brand new machine which we then proceed to disassemble and use at about 2% of its full capacity for the rest of our lives. In order to go back to full speed, we need to reassemble our thinking and feeling brains and get the two sides working synergistically.

I think the old saying that the road to success is paved with good intentions is out of date. Indeed, I believe the road to *failure* is paved with good intentions, and we travel over them in reckless fashion on our way to an "average" life.

Here's a famous illustration. There are three frogs sitting on a lily pad. One of them decides to jump off the pad into the water. How many frogs are then left on the lily pad? If you answered "two" you're actually one away from the answer. There are still three left on the pad, because one only *decided* to jump off, but *did not*! Decision, not preceded by action is absolutely worthless! The same idea holds true for intentions. Without action, they too have no value whatsoever.

The word "action" is a self-fulfilling word...when scrambled it becomes I-act-on, a phrase that can bring excitement to your otherwise humdrum life. Of course, with further scrambling we also get I-no-act! The choice is ultimately *yours to make*!

Getting back to 55 MPH. If you break the law, you then *brake* for the patrol car...and pay for your "error". Thus, it is in the universe, which has its own laws. Whenever we break Universal Law, we must pay the fine. It can be paid financially, physically, mentally or spiritually...but it must be paid. The further we "drive" from the natural order of things, the more they can and will break down for us, as does our car when we mistreat it. Try putting milk (a very healthy drink) into your gas tank, and watch it get very "sick".

A hefty dose of introspection will reveal to us the laws of the universe...the ones that are good for us. Take time out daily to find out how you fit into the scheme of things, and watch your life take on new dimensions.

One of my "bon-mots" on the subject says: "Meditate, don't medicate!" Now that Washington tells us we may hit a trillion dollars per year in health costs by the year 2000...it behooves us not to become part of this unbelievable statistic.

# Fifty Seven

# Amazing People

A popular magazine came out with an issue dedicated solely to what they referred to as "Amazing Americans". Included among them were achievers heroes and underdogs, who, the magazine claimed, beat the "odds" with brains, guts and luck. We read about the California farmer who was shooting for a 500-pound pumpkin; a 12-year old child who climbed the tallest mountain in the United States (Mt. McKinley); the 61-year old man who finally became an attorney after failing the bar exam 47 times in 25 years. We rejoiced when we read about the baby born at 27 weeks and weighing 9.9 ounces (that's right, ounces), lived and is now a small but spunky child of two. We cheered when we read about the sky diver who jumped at 10,500 feet and both her main parachute, as well as the backup *failed to open*... and she survived the fall. Finally, we marveled at the 82-year old inventor-farmer who has never paid for electricity because his 100-acre farm is totally energy self sufficient.

I wrote the editorial "we" on all of the above, but frankly, should have written "you" because I found nothing miraculous about any of the "amazing" feats. Please don't misunderstand. I give *full credit* to these people for their accomplishments, but I don't believe they "beat the odds". Rather, they are the ones who make up the "odds". To my way of thinking, it is amazing that so few of us make up these numbers when we have all inherited the same "will to win" at birth. Being a part of universal intelligence, we *all* have the ability to tap into this vast reservoir of human potential. Yet, most of us go through life dipping into it with a teaspoon when we should be using gigantic cauldrons, thus guaranteeing that a fair share of the unlimited resources in the universe would be ours to use as we go through life.

I'm sure these exceptional human beings would all agree that two of the most important qualities they developed early in life were a positive mental attitude and a powerful will to win. Combined with persistence, this trio of human strengths enabled these wonderful folks to be written up in the magazine as winners and movers.

Over a century ago, Ralph Waldo Emerson wrote the following: "Hitch Your Wagon to a Star!" Looks as though some of us do exactly that, and reap the benefits of higher accomplishments in their sojourn on earth. Human potential being what it is, there is very little to stop us from joining these few "gifted" individuals, since we use a minimum of what we are innately born with.

We should develop a new curriculum to teach us that we have the greatness germ already in us, and need to nurture it both at home and away from it.

# Fifty Eight

# It Works .... Always!

Contrary to popular belief and usage, the word "repent" is not only used with regards to "sinning"; another meaning is changing one's mind. This means to take a diametrically opposed view of a long-held belief, based on new information or a new feeling re: the subject matter involved. The beauty of it is that when the change is made mentally, physical conditions change as well. We see this often when dealing with sick patients. Those who change their minds about living, and fighting the illness which threatens to kill them live; conversely, if they give up and decide not to fight, they die, fulfilling their own worst prophesy.

This idea works on the attitudes we bring to life, as well as physiological changes we want to make. Since thoughts represent the mental equivalent of our physical status, there is a strong connection between what we think and what happens in our bodies. I have a dear friend who years ago co-hosted a prosperity seminar with me. At the time, she was easily one of the greatest men-hating cynics I knew. She had been dealt some bad karma via the men in her life, and developed a deep-seated hatred for all men. She had been used and abused for so long that she now accepted the fact that no man would ever fill a permanent niche in her life. Since prosperity is a by-product of a happy, hate-free life, she missed on that count as well. A young grandmother, she thought life a bummer, and lived mostly for her family, minus a man.

I phoned her last week for some information, and thought for a while I had the wrong number. Her body language came through the telephone line, and I had to step back to avoid being bowled over by her new enthusiasm. Her laughter sounded like a crystal chandelier, gently swinging in the wind...and literally *sparkled*! I decided this was worth a personal visit.

One week later, my wife and I showed up at her place of business, a futon store, where we met her "new and much improved" husband. It seems that after all the years of anger and hatred for the opposite sex, a friend had convinced her that she was only getting back what she was sending out...and her life would not change until she changed her basic philosophy about men. Well, my friend "repented" (i.e., changed her mind and feelings) and less than *three weeks later*, met the man of her younger and more innocent dreams. They married earlier this summer while on a futon convention in Virginia, and *I know* they will live happily thereafter. You just have to see the sparkle in their eyes coupled with her uncanny laughter to know she is free of the negative past, and looking forward to a wondrous future with her man. His past story paralleled hers, and is also forgotten.

# *Fifty Nine*

# Fear

I was sitting on my sunny porch on a Saturday morning, waiting to be picked up by a friend for our weekly breakfast. In front of me were several pots of petunias. Suddenly, a wasp alighted on one of them and began to flutter from one flower to another. It was soon joined by a bee, also intent on gathering as much pollen as it could carry. The two seemed oblivious of each other, as well as of me. It was a very peaceful scene, with not a single thought of fear among the three of us.

Later, after breakfast, I went on my usual walk, carrying two dumbbells, and wearing my Sony tape player, listening to motivational tapes. A dog, unknown to me, came over as I passed his home...wagged his tail, and we became friends. He walked with me to the end of his block, wagged a final goodbye, and left me. Once again, fear never entered our peaceful encounter.

I have reached the point in my life where I understand fear as a self-inflicted psychological trauma...brought on by previous negative conditioning. Since the animal and insect kingdoms do not deal with life on a human level, they do not inherit fear as part of their early conditioning.

Wouldn't it be wonderful if our children were brought up with no previous fears, passed along almost genetically by their families, with a clean slate so to speak, and with their *own* set of crayons, thus able to draw from their own personal experiences, not someone else's angry, frightened scribblings.

Fear, a wise man once said, is faith turned inside out. I have full faith in an orderly, meaningful universe where fear does not exist except if we choose to acknowledge it.

Fear of other human beings is in reality, fear of our own insecurities or inferiority, manifesting itself against innocent victims. Fear paralyzes the creative spark we are born with, and interferes with the development of our greater talents and abilities. Fear turns to anger, hatred, frustration, and ultimately transforms itself into psychosomatic illnesses, most of which we already *fear!*

Since we are born unafraid as children, I would like to add a final quote to this vignette. From Mencius...372-289 B.C.: "The great man (woman) is he who does not lose his child's heart!"

# Pancakes

For eight years, my wife made wonderful pancakes every Sunday. I mean those thin ones that could pass for crepes suzettes or palachintas (for you Europeans). I love them, yet had to give them up as a weekly treat. You see, several months ago, my wife inadvertently said to me: "If it wasn't for those damned pancakes you insist upon every Sunday, I'd be able to get my work done at least two hours earlier...and enjoy my weekend more!" My first reply was, "I thought you loved making them for us. After all, it's a good time for family bonding". Said my beloved, "I hate doing them!" End of story. My marriage is certainly more important than Sunday pancakes. The point of this story is: "Why did it take my wife eight years to let me know how she felt about the pancakes?" I teach communication skills, and yet must have missed her body signals for all these years. Just goes to show what happens when you're too close to the problem. True to her nature, my wife decided to meet me half-way (by her reckoning). Instead of 50+ times per year, I now get pancakes on my birthday, the 4th of July (which declares her independence from them), Labor Day (reminding me of the work involved), Thanksgiving (and she should give thanks), Christmas and New Year. A perfect six-pack of pancake days.

I must add a P.S.

I do watch for body signals a little more closely. I hope she doesn't feel the same about our weekly, Friday raviolis. Perhaps if she doesn't read this, my raviolis are safe.

My lesson here is simple; if my philosophy is worth sharing with lecture and seminar attendees, I had better use it myself at home...or else 'twill be a classic case of the shoemaker whose children walk around barefoot!

I guess I had better practice at home what I teach elsewhere, because if it works at home *I know* I'm on the right track.

I'm always telling people our Creator gave us two eyes, two ears and only one mouth. This means we should see and hear four times as much as *speak*. Whenever I remember this concept and apply it at home, I find I stay out of trouble. (Do you have any idea how tough that is for a professional *speaker* to do?)

Live and learn may be a nice platitude...but I believe that "love and learn" works better in any one-on-one situation.

# Sixty One

# 40th Anniversary

No, not mine. My total wedded years to date add up to 20, but I don't think that qualifies as an anniversary, since 20 is the sum total of my marriages. What we did was celebrate my in-laws' 40th. To each other. And isn't that going to be happening less and less as we move into the "enlightened" 21st Century?

Anyway, the celebration took place in a beautiful inn over 200 years old. The food, ambiance and service were superb. The previous year I had done two seminars in that fine establishment on Customer Service...and it showed as our waiter and waitress catered to our every whim.

A few minor glitches developed in an otherwise perfect affair. First, their "best man" and his wife had to cancel coming at the last minute because of a bachelor party being given for their son that same night. Then, the groom's sister and brother-in-law had to leave early for her 40th high school reunion, also scheduled for that night.

The other glitches were of a more humorous nature. The first came quite unexpectedly. As we all began to sing the traditional Happy Anniversary song, one of the bride's sisters stopped us cold and began to sing the song in another tempo. Since we were unfamiliar with this version of the song, she ended up doing a solo, with us as her audience.

The second glitch topped the charts for humor. The room was quiet at the moment, without the music from the sound system. The bride's mother, matriarch of the clan, had just received her dessert, a truly inspired apple strudel (a specialty of the house). She lifted the thin crust of her strudel, then exclaimed in a loud voice, "Why the hell do they put raisins in these cakes?" The whole room shook with laughter. She then proceeded to tell us that she will eat raisins out of those "little boxes"...but never in cakes and pies.

She capped off the occasion when the gifts were opened, and it was discovered that her card was not signed. We thought she might want to reuse it another time, and suggested she leave it that way. But...with the "Why the hell do they put raisins in these cakes?" still ringing in her ears, she decided to sign the card...and a good time was had by all!

Frankly, I can't wait for their 80th anniversary. I've already put in a reservation with the inn. After all, we know it will still be around for another century or two.

P.S. After the party, a great mound of raisins was found on Grandma's dessert plate!

# Sixty Two.

# Motivation

In a recent year, the new college graduates were asked to define their #1 problem as they readied themselves for the outside business world. Fully three out of every four polled answered with the same hyphenated word: *self-confidence!* What a terrible indictment on the educational system, as well as the home environment the majority of students come from. As Shakespeare would say, "A pox on *both* your houses!"

A lack of self-confidence equals a poor self-image, as well as a low self-esteem. All are interrelated, and show that a weak learning foundation has been poured into these graduates' minds, beginning in the home and culminating in the higher school system. All of the above eventually lead to a low or non-existent level of personal motivation, which is *crucial* to success in the business world. Fortunately, all is not lost. It's been said that where there's life there's hope, and this holds true where motivation is concerned.

An article in Reader's Digest (circa 1975) confirms the fact that if we change how we think about *ourselves*, as well as our *surroundings*...we can change motivation and improve performance! The study took 25 years, and was done at Harvard University. That gives the research powerful recognition and thus, acceptance. If the new graduate does not want to go into a job with a negative attitude, i.e.:

Moody Monday...Tough Tuesday...Worried Wednesday...Thankless Thursday...and Fearful/Frantic Friday...

it stands to reason he/she must change his attitude toward himself and his surroundings. The best method is to replace the old mentality with a new and stronger philosophy...thus effectively negating the past, and brightening the immediate future. The replacement can take several forms. These include reading the great books of the world...seeing the biographies of those whose lives were enhanced by positive changes (via the movies or T.V. or video-cassettes)...going to New Age seminars...in fact, *anything* which will change our preconceived ideas of what this world is all about, and our role in it.

We all accept the fact that we were born to *win*...but programmed to become average. The trick is to make a decision to change, and then implement it with *action steps!*

This is one way to avoid joining another awful statistic: Only half of new employees in America remain on the job as long as nine months. This figure from the U.S. Department of Labor.

The Dale Carnegie Foundation told us many years ago that our Job Aptitude accounts for only 15% of our success, and our Mental Attitude accounts for the rest...*85% of success!*

# Sixty Three

# Eudaimonism

This is about a trio of giants! All three preeminent in the humanities. A common thread runs through these three lives. Although they are separated in time by almost 25 centuries...469 B.C. to present, their philosophical ideals are as fresh as today's picked roses.

The first giant is named Socrates...and his philosophy is best summed up in one word: Eudaimonism! This theory promotes the idea that only virtuous actions produce lasting happiness, or that a person's self-interest is best served by always doing the right thing.

The second is a contemporary of ours. He is also the acknowledged world authority on *stress*...having written over 30 books, plus 1500 technical articles on the subject. He is, of course, the eminent Dr. Hans Selye, of the University of Montreal. His best response to the problem of stress in society is what he calls "altruistic egoism". This concept involves the *selfish* hoarding of the love of our neighbor and peer as we *earn it through unselfish acts* performed for others!

Last, but certainly not least, we present our final giant...whose name itself takes him out of the ordinary. In his current bestseller "*FLOW*, the Psychology of Optimal Experience" Mihaly Csikszentmihalyi (pronounced SHIK-sent-mee-HIGH, if you dare to attempt it) summarizes his theory on what he calls the autotelic self. Literally it means a "self that has self-contained goals". If they are self-contained, they must come from within. Within lies our intuition, inspiration and insight. These are all good qualities inherited at birth. When used with the outside world, they can only lead to "winners-all-around" results.

Have you noticed the similarities in the three systems, all designed to help us lead happy, stress-free lives? It seems that even time has not dimmed the power of this philosophy...which was also so eloquently stated 2,000 years ago: "It is more blessed to give than to receive!" Perhaps he should have added..."because to give is to *receive*!"

Obviously, if you take these world experts seriously, we are born to love, and give. Since nature abhors a vacuum, the more of it we create in our lives, the more will come back to refill us.

We will then lead eustress-laden existences, eustress being the good and healthy kind of stress, designed to help us grow into full maturity.

Distress can kill, while eustress heals. The choice, ultimately, is ours to make.

# Sixty Four

# Academic Independence

If Henry David Thoreau were alive today, and about to choose a school of higher learning to attend, I believe he would pass up Harvard. Instead, he would end up at Hillside College in Michigan. I say this because it is always ranked as one of the top small colleges in the United States. "Independent Excellence" could easily be its motto, since it is the only college left in America that has refused (for its 146 years of existence) to accept federal funds...and thereby federal control! As I'm sure Thoreau would have said, academic freedom and financial independence are like the two sides of the same coin, *inseparable*.

I await their monthly journal (305,000 worldwide circulation at this time) with great anticipation, because its contents are not stained with the federal imprimatur. It has to kowtow to no one, thus maintaining its academic standings legitimately. This is the kind of institution which has made our country great by keeping government support out of it. Government support always has political strings attached to it, thus creating a puppet regime out of an otherwise honorable institution.

Hillsdale College received the *top award* from the John Templeton Foundation in 1991...out of 1300 colleges competing for that most prestigious title. There were 87 finalists on the 1991 Honor Rolls..."For Character Building Colleges and For Free Enterprise Teaching." It is not by accident that Hillsdale College named its monthly publication IMPRIMUS (Latin for "in the first place") in 1972.

Voluntary support is the only fund-raising method used by the college to keep it out of federal hands (claws?).

To call itself a non-profit organization is a misnomer, since the students going there will profit enormously by not being fettered because of government regulations. I believe these are the graduates to watch as they invade U.S. business with a clear conscience and powerful academic credentials.

"That government is best which governs not at all", comes from the pen of Henry David Thoreau. It's time to rethink the role filled by politicians, and send many of them packing. Sometimes, *less is better*!

My proverbial hat is off to Hillsdale College. May it become a role model for other schools of higher learning to emulate.

# Sixty Five

# Tuna

The story is told of a man sitting next to his friend and co-worker. As he unwraps his lunch and looks at it, he turns to his friend and says, "Damn! Tuna fish again! I hate tuna fish." His friend replies thusly, "Why don't you ask your wife to fix you something else for lunch. I'm sure she wouldn't mind." Sadly, the answer came back in a low monotone, "I can't ask my wife. I've been fixing my own lunch for the past 25 years!"

Question. Have you been fixing your own lunch (life) the same way all the time...and then complaining at the unhappy results? Life gives you exactly what your menu calls for. You cannot change the restaurant you eat in, but you can change what you bring for "lunch".

Look around you and see what others are bringing to eat. If you see something you prefer to yours, don't ask for a "trade". No one can trade his life for yours. Instead, find out what he/she is doing right, and get the recipe for yourself. Try out the new meal, and, if it feels right inside you, it's for you. There's that "gut feeling" (pun intended) coming to rescue you from a continuing life of despair and possibly hell. The key of course is to make the decision, albeit traumatic, to add gusto to your life. Healthy trauma can replace old belief systems if acted upon with positive expectancy. Learning to love yourself can be a lifelong quest, but it's worth it. Beginning the journey with faltering steps, you will quickly turn them into long, confident strides as you pursue success and happiness...and *catch them!*

T.U.N.A. in my lexicon stands for Totally Unacceptable Negative Attitude. Negatives belong in a darkroom, not in your day-to-day activities. Sometimes our negativity has been passed along to us by our parents, who got it from their parents, who got it from their parents...ad infinitum. It can be passed along almost genetically for centuries, *until* someone applies a brake and says no more! A new branch of the family is now formed, with only positives growing from it.

Will you be the one breaking the chain of mental slavery, or will you pass the "baton" to another, who will then streak to victory? Making the right choice is like deciding to eat from the Group A or Group B from a Chinese menu. You must live with your choice once it is made.

Life is like photography. You can take one negative, turn it around, and develop many positives from it. Don't see the world "through a glass, darkly". Use instead, your inner light, and you will never be mistaken for the person of whom it is said, "He/she brightens up a room by *leaving it!*"

# Sixty Six

# Remembrances

My parents, brother and I were among the first refugees to come to the United States during World War II. We arrived in New York Harbor in April 1943, from Casablanca, French Morocco. For months, when I walked the streets of New York City, I ducked out of sight each time I saw a uniformed policeman. He reminded me of the Nazi officers who used to visit Casablanca, and it took a long time before I understood that here were the good guys, and I had nothing to be afraid of.

My mother reacted differently with regards to our past as displaced persons. She carefully stapled the labels which hung from pillowcases and upholstered chairs so that they would not come off by accident. The labels which read, "*do not remove under penalty of law!*"

We may laugh about these needless fears now, but I ask my readers the following: How many of you still live with the fear of the "law" deeply ingrained in your subconscious. Law meaning both rules and regulations, as well as the religious restrictions placed on us by the "middlemen" of organized religion in order to *control* us. Control by fear is, after all, the best way to insure the financial well-being of the controllers.

I have studied various religions for many years, and have reached what I found to be a common denominator with all of them. Beginning my research with a quote from "The Teaching for Merikare" (king of Heracleopolis) C.2135-2040 B.C. He wrote to his son, Merikare: "Serve God, that He may do the like for you..." Almost 4,000 years later, we find the same attitude in the writings of teachers of New Thought, which in reality, is Old Thought brought into the 20th century. Once again, Creative Intelligence is linked to goodness...and not fire and brimstone.

If you are not as happy as you hoped to be at this stage of your life, examine your religious beliefs for spiritual integrity. If it is lacking...you may be dealing with a case of spiritual bankruptcy. If anger, hatred and vengeance are taught as moralistic fodder for your hungry mind...run like hell, or perhaps *from hell*. For as Confucius said (551-479 B.C.): "What you do not want done to yourself, do not do to others!" Add to this what another wise Chinese philosopher once wrote: "He who seeks revenge on another should dig *two* graves."

If remembrances are painful, use them as a springboard to a better future than your past has been. I choose to learn from my past, but will no longer suffer over it. My past is over!...as yours is. Use your emotions to build a better present and future. Do not waste them on what has already occurred in your life. *Emotions* are precious. To me, the word means Enthusiasm in Motion!

# Sixty Seven

# Left + Right

In my previous vignettes, as well as my major articles on Positive Living, I allude to the different sides of the brain, i.e., left and right hemispheres. My reason is to impress upon you the importance of understanding the basic functions of both sides of the bicameral brain. Only thus can a person learn to make full use of his/her potential for success; success being defined as the proper balance between positive thinking and positive feeling. Our analytical self takes care of the "thinking" part, and our emotional self is in charge of the "feeling" part. In 19 out of every 20 persons, the thinking/analytical is handled in the left brain, while the feeling/emotional is covered by the right.

Unless a connection is made via the corpus colassum...a bridge consisting of hundreds of millions of cells situated in between the hemispheres, we are working at less than half our mental power. When each side has different goals for you, it sets up what we call a self-defeating situation, wherein left and right brains are actually fighting for control of your mind...thus frustrating your efforts at living with "peace of mind"!

Why bring up such a mundane subject at this time? Well, a recent study was made by the Sociology Department at Duke University on the concept of peace of mind. Their conclusion: Much unhappiness stems from a morbid preoccupation with *past mistakes and failures*! This means we are using our "feeling" brain to bring back negative emotions...without the benefit of our "rational" side to erase these bad events from our lives permanently. Whole-brain experiences are what we're really after.

One car company which understood this concept ran a series of two-page ads, designed to appeal to both types of customers. One ad was titled, "A car for the left side of your brain" (left page). The other ad, on the right page of the ad was titled, "A car for the right side of your brain". The left page was full of print, for rational and analytical reading. The right page only had a picture of the car (Saab), leaving your imagination to do the rest.

My best description for the left or right-brain dominants is to visualize two people sitting in front of two bowls of alphabet soup. The dominant left-brainer will eat the letters in the soup *alphabetically*, while the dominant right-brainer will eat the same letters by words conjured up on the spot.

I always recommend at my lectures and seminars that those who are extremists on either brain side, begin to dip into the unused portion. The results can be *spectacular*! They will bring new dimensions to your living...resulting in greater peace of mind!

# Sixty Eight

# Laughter

"When the first baby laughed for the first time, the laugh broke into a thousand pieces and they all went skipping about..." Quoted from "Peter Pan" by J.M. Barrie (1810-1891). Laughter in children has not changed much since this was written, but has become somewhat of a rarity in today's adults. Latest reportable data on this merry subject reveals the facts that very young children laugh approximately 500 times per day. As their size and age increases, their laughter decreases. As adults they now average 15 laughs per day.

If we accept the fact that "a merry heart doeth good", why do we diminish this very cost-effective method of improving our health. Not only does a good laugh give you an internal message, but it also helps relieve stress. The mind experts tell us that by age 30, we have amassed 6,000,000,000,000 (that's right, six trillion) memory bits in our subconscious bio-computer. Since most of these occurred at younger ages, when we were just evolving into thinking beings...they were of a negative nature, when we resisted much of the training.

By the way, I don't agree with the "when you laugh, the world laughs with you...when you cry, you cry alone" philosophy. There are times I laugh just because it's great to be alive!...that's when I laugh alone, since this is a highly personal time for me. I think the trick is to go back into a child-like (vs. childish) attitude towards life. Only then can we hope to "up the ante" and get closer to the old magic of 500 laughs per day. A healthy dose of self-love is also indicated at this time, since this will definitely guarantee an increase in laughability. (Laughability is not in my dictionary. It should be, since the ability to laugh has become a rare gift in adults.)

The trick in recapturing this precious gift is to begin a program first mentioned by the Greeks 2,000 years ago, when they penned the now classic phrase "Know Thyself!" After self knowledge comes *self-acceptance*...as you *are*! Even with the fat thighs, pimples and wrinkles. You then use the acceptance part as a diving board, from which you will jump head-first into a new and better future. By accepting yourself, you will also begin to forgive yourself for *past misdeeds*...which have no bearing on your current life. As long as you *change* from now on you can let go of several trillion "bad-bits" which your thoughts constantly trip over, thereby limiting your laugh quotient. To repeat the key; you must begin to change from this moment on...thereby earning the right to laugh as children do when they are still full of innocence. "Laugh, and your world laughs with you!" makes more sense than the old platitude.

# Sixty Nine

# Nay-bors/Aye-bors

You probably guessed that I took a lot of poetic license as I wrote the two title words. They mean Neighbors (negative ones) vs. Positive ones, Aye-(yes)bors. After all, aren't these two types the ones we encounter most when we move into a new area or new home?

In my younger, immature years, I consistently moved into new apartments with very poor quality neighbors. Later, as I grew up, I found that when I relocated into new quarters, the neighbors I met were quite sociable and civilized. It took me a while longer to understand that this was no coincidence. Instead, I realized that each time I moved...I took *me along with me*! What a revelation that turned out to be. I understood then that I did not leave my fears, insecurities and prejudices behind, along with my former address. Instead, they hung on to me like a flea on a dog. This simply meant that in order to see the change in others, I had to do the initial changing. As I changed my self-image, I saw my new neighbors differently as well. As I improved, so did they.

Today, I meet *all new people* with an attitude of Positive Expectancy, and they usually fulfill my unspoken prophecy. I still think of my old nay-bors occasionally, and wonder if they also discovered the secret and changed their attitudes toward their new neighbors.

I recall having the philosophy of "Always expect the worst and you'll never be disappointed!" for many years, due to my negative upbringing. Guess what? I was not disappointed. Life gave me exactly what I expected of it. I did not then see the connection between my reaping and my sowing. I have now changed the seeds I am always sowing...and fully expect a much better crop than I had in the past.

What I have been saying in this vignette can best be told thusly. If you want to know what you bring to your new neighborhood, look closely at your new neighbors. If they treat you negatively, they are mirroring your attitudes, and you will have to deal with nay-bors. If instead, you are treated with respect and recognition, it means you are helping them to become Aye-bors...Positive new friends, who once again are mirroring *your attitude*!

It sounds to me like a simple case of "doing unto others *before* they will do unto you". And that's one of the great secrets of loving yourself, because if you give it away first, you're creating a "love vacuum" which others will be glad to fill for you. Kinda like a lover's dream, wouldn't you agree?

# Seventy

# Prosperity

Just finished doing a talk for a local business association. It was called "How to Develop a Prosperity Consciousness During Difficult Times!"...a lecture I have given many times this year, as we continue to accept and participate in the "recession". Before my lecture, I like to wander around, meeting people and listening to their latest outlook on business. This gives me a good handle on the group, and I can further personalize my talk to meet their specific needs. Well, it seems this group, like most others I addressed this year, was P.O.'d (Problem-Oriented), and the place echoed with negative feelings. The most-used word, in its negative connotation was "enthusiasm"...or to be more correct, the *lack of it* on the job.

Once enthusiasm (God residing within us) is gone, we turn into veritable zombies...the walking dead. It seems as though many of those present were trying to upstage others by insisting their lot was the worst possible in the room. The main thrust of their discontent was the fact that their boss (to some, boss spelled backwards now meant "Double S.O.B.") wanted *more work* out of them, without paying extra for it.

Since Stanford University's research in the '80's showed that the average American uses 2% of his/her full potential...it would seem that the demand for more work is not unreasonable, especially in these trying times. The problem is that in these same '80's, the economy went so smoothly, that many of us "coasted" through them, running into a brick wall when 1990 showed up on our calendars. I reminded my audience for over 40 minutes, that *enthusiasm* is an inside job, and highly personal. Also, it is extremely catching because most of us need a daily supply of it, as we do Vitamin C. Thus, the best way to *keep* enthusiasm is to continually *give it away*, creating the vacuum for more.

Prosperity means economic well-being. Enthusiasm is emotional well-being, and is the catalyst to further financial success. It comes before prosperity in the dictionary, and should be the first quality you exhibit in front of your peers, co-workers and family. The ripples enthusiastic people create travel ad infinitum, as they are passed along from person to person, infecting them with a new "joi de vivre".

Another definition of enthusiasm is to be "inspired"...i.e., to be divinely guided. With that kind of leadership, how can you go wrong.

I also recommend that the attendees go back to developing more of their people skills, because eventually, prosperity depends on the number of workers they can motivate to greater productivity. *A true* win-win scenario!

# Seventy One

# How Are You Doing?

Since I stress self-knowledge throughout my vignettes, I feel it would be a great idea to find out exactly where you are right now...before you continue on your journey to greater achievement. The following is a self-test I give to my seminar attendees when the time permits. Please take the test now and answer the questions as quickly as possible, since intuitive input needs little thinking, and your first answer will generally be the correct one.

**GETTING TO KNOW YOU!**

Please answer questions 1 through 4 with one of the following:

Happy, Content, Unhappy

1. How do you feel about your current financial situation?
2. Your job/occupation?
3. Your family life?
4. Yourself?
   A. How's your Self-Esteem?
   B. What do you like and admire most about yourself?
   C. What do you dislike and hate most about yourself?
   D. Are you satisfied with your present level of success?
   E. Do you truly feel appreciated by peers for what you are?
   F. Do you think that most of your problems today are caused by other people's attitudes...or yours?
5. What 3 problems in your life would you like to solve first?
6. If you could change situations, what would you do?
7. How much would you like to earn next year?
8. What's stopping you...or who?
9. What would be your first step to solve this dilemma?
10. Are you ready now to forget your negative past, forgive your errors and those of others, and really begin the first day of the rest of your life?

I end the test with the forgiveness statement because this is the most important stumbling block most of us will ever encounter in our quest for personal and financial success. Past angers, hatreds and frustrations with others form a solid wall between who are are and what we want to become! The only way to break our self-built wall down permanently is to relegate the ancient, archaic, negative part to the Museum of Forgotten Memories. Once you forgive yourself and others, you will get off the local and hop on the Success Express, as your new self-image takes charge of your career.

# Seventy Two.

# Bagels

This just happened two hours ago, as I went for my daily walk. I ended up at a mall, which has a bagel "emporium". Since I believe in a good breakfast, to "break-my-fast", I went inside. This is what occurred, and why I am putting it down on paper.

I ordered "two eggs, over medium, one well-done poppy bagel, with a light shmear of butter, and a coffee with milk and Sweet-and-Low in it". This is what was repeated, and given to me: "Did you want eggs over medium?" After I reconfirmed the eggs, I also received the following: One *lightly-done* sesame bagel, very *heavy* on the butter. Hey, that's batting 1,000...three errors for three special requests.

There was no else at the counter at the time, so that my server's attention was fully on **ME**. Or was it? The word "listen" also spells "silent". There must have been much on her mind at the moment I appeared, because I know I intruded in her *intalk*. I teach listening skills, and refer to the "psychobabble" we are often engaged in when supposedly listening to someone speaking to us. We tune out the outside "noise", being completely immersed in our own personal dramas, which we go over and over in our minds.

If the experts are right...and they include the American Management Association, the inimitable Leo Buscaglia, plus scores of publications (business and personal) then over 85% of us agree that *communications* is the most important talent we bring into any one-on-one situation. Communication consists of at least two people, a sender and a receiver. Both must agree on what's being communicated. Perhaps if I had asked the bagel-lady, "Do I have your *undivided* attention?", I might have gotten one, or possibly two out of three correct items. As a hopeless optimist, I see my bagel as half-full of butter, instead of my bagel runneth over.

Listening is showing love for the other person. Generally, we will be *listened to* in direct proportion to the listening *we do*. But we must learn to *listen first*, because we can't change people. What does change is their *attitude* toward us...because their human nature demands that they do unto us as they are being done unto. If they are rude the first time around, they may be testing us to see if we fit in with the other misfits they have to deal with on a daily basis.

My personal credo tells me to let the rudeness pass, and treat them with respect, "above and beyond the call of duty". It will work if given enough time with the same people, as they begin to realize that you mean to treat them respectfully. Last year I was bumped upward twice from coach to first class on American Airlines out of Chicago to Long Island, because I showed respect by listening carefully to one ticket-counter lady and one flight attendant, and offering empathy as well for their difficulties. My flight to Long Island had to be diverted to LaGuardia because of torrential rains, and one large male passenger was berating the ticket counter attendant, using abusive language. I told her she was doing an excellent job handling the crisis and to pay no mind to the jerk. The second time, I volunteered to move to another seat because we had too many people in our row (young children who needed individual seating), and they needed to stay together. Two simple kindnesses, and I had two excellent return trips in first class. (No undercooked and over-buttered bagels on these trips).

*Success is the child of auducity*

Benjamin Disreli

# Seventy Three

# Diogenes

What's wrong with people today? When the University of Michigan queried 15,000 people as to their favorite gripe...99.8% checked off the same multiple choice answer: "Nobody listens to me!" Last night, after doing a one-hour presentation on "How to Develop a Prosperity Consciousness During Difficult Times!", I wished I had the lantern Diogenes used centuries ago to find an honest man.

My talk used an acronym, and part of it was the ticklish issue of *ethics*. After discussing honesty, integrity and ethics in the work-place, and getting *full agreement* from the audience on their importance today, here's what happened. A sales rep decided to purchase my new 4-cassette tape program, which stresses the above mentioned qualities, and tried to rip off New York State of its legitimate tax on the tapes. He was putting his ethics on the line for $3.00! What price honesty, I ask? Why wasn't he listening? He heard me, but was not listening. Obviously his intalk was more important and influential than the message I was conveying to the audience.

Is it any wonder then that Diogenes (400-325 B.C.) was known by his contemporaries as Diogenes the Cynic. Instead of his antiquated lantern, we could use a laser light, but I'm not sure we would have better success at finding the honest person with it. I don't mean to imply that there are no people left with integrity, but I feel too often it has become a "gray area"...no longer black or white.

The rule for finding out what is truly honest is simple. If you are busy justifying and rationalizing (to yourself) why you did something...then it is at least the "gray area" of ethics, and possibly black.

Wasn't it Shakespeare who said "To Thine *Own* Self be True...etc." We possess a mental governor which tells us deep inside when we screw up on anything. We must learn to listen to that "still, small voice". It will guide us, if we allow it, to a greater sense of *self-worth*. This in turn will help us reach personal and financial goals we once thought impossible, because as we all know, "As a person thinketh in his *heart*...so is he!"

Being incurably optimistic about the future of the human race, I will leave Diogenes where he belongs, *in the past*....as I venture into the future, encouraging people to reach for new levels of honesty. Eventually, this may actually save their lives.

# Seventy Four

# Self-Criticism

Last week I was doing motivational counseling with two clients. I asked them to make two lists for me. The first was an appraisal of their personal assets and liabilities, i.e., positives and negatives. The second list was to describe the other person who was a co-worker and friend. Truth-in-writing was insisted upon. The following are some interesting results, based on a few of their answers:

A - wrote:
**I am** a procrastinator
I don't like criticism
I hate to follow up on things
I blow up too easily
I yell too much

B - (wrote about A):
**You are:**
caring, concerned,
emotional, funny,
intelligent, cute,
loving and happy

B - wrote:
I am fat, overweight
I am not good-looking
I am not efficient, scatterbrain
I am shy
I am opinionated
I am not smart enough
I have a low self-esteem
I am lazy, a procrastinator
And the negative list continued..

A - (wrote about B)
sweet
loving
caring
honest
loving
trustworthy
happy
sincere

Are we blind, deaf and dumb...or do we enjoy this self-flagellation, and what it does to our Self-Image. Why would we deliberately find more negatives in our lives...while others, who are close to us, can see and appreciate our better qualities? They say that self-praise stinks; I think it is absolutely essential to good mental health, but it must be sincere, based on true feelings about yourself. Some things just can't be faked. Your self-esteem will grow geometrically as you increase self-praise.

Remember, there are no perfect people. Just people trying to discard their imperfections. The best way to do this is to spend your thinking/ feeling time on the side of optimism. This will help create the conditions you want in your life, as the subconscious now begins to be solutions-oriented and steers away from problems.

Make your own list today...Right Now!  Read it first thing in the morning and just before retiring.  Only your positive qualities must be listed. You've already spent enough time on the negatives you thought you had to drag behind you for the rest of your life.  Each day is a New Beginning, with new chances for personal growth.

*The only people that I have ever known*
*to have no problems are in the cemetary*

Dr. Norman Vincent Peale

# Seventy Five

# Teenage Screw Up

Well, looks like I did it to myself. Probably lost any chance at making the front cover of Teenage Magazine. It seems I managed to alienate some of my son's peers (and especially peerettes) who call regularly on the phone. After hearing "Hello, is Joe home?" once too often, I decided to improve telecommunications. I gently began asking the ladies (who were a majority) to please identify themselves by first name for me when I answered the rings. After all, it could be Barbara Bush calling, or a witch to invite my son to a coven.

That's when it began. The callers are now hanging up on me, and I have become anathema on the phone. The new pariah now speaks into dead phones. It seems that only adults are expected to show a little respect on the phone. At least that's what I have taught in 35 states when I do my *the very best telephone skills* full day seminars. I always recommend using your name when telephoning someone. I felt I was not asking too much by having 15-year old "adults" calling my home, and saying, "Hello, this is Judy...is Joe home?"

Anyhow, the night we discussed this new turn of events in my home (my wife agrees with my son), the T.V. news reported that almost 3,000 teenagers were killed by other teenagers wielding the new favorite status symbol...a 9mm handgun. No respect for life, much less for the feelings of another human being. I feel I deserve the *respect* I ask on the phone. I don't even ask them to call me Mr. Weisel...(Are you out of your mind?) There is enough data to back me up when I say that respect in the home is where it all begins. Later, this respect is transferred to all levels of authority, or *anarchy* would prevail.

I like his young friends, and I'm sorry I am now the ogre in their young, immature eyes. I prided myself on treating them all with respect when they called. Reciprocity is not in their high school dictionary. Truly a shame, since respect for others begets respect for us.

In some ways I'll continue to be old-fashioned until I leave this earth for greener pastures. It may be tough at times, but guess what? *I respect myself*...and sometimes that's all one needs to feel good about himself. I know my son's friends will never become the 9mm-toting kind, but I believe respect is like pregnancy. You either are or you aren't. Respect is definitely a mark of a healthy Self-Esteem. Isn't that what we all strive for?

If you ever have the chance to call me, you'll always get an enthusiastic "Good.....This is Jacques Weisel speaking!"

And for now, this is Jacques Weisel, signing off.

# Seventy Six

# 540-HUGS

Yes, 540-hugs is the phone number to call if you are hugless and want to change that status. Now, I'm a believer in hugs, and try to get my share as often as possible. As a matter of fact, I have built my own HUG acronym...Healthy Unconditional Giving! I also feel it is much better to "hug" than "drug". The ad includes *Guys*Girls*Gays*Lesbians*...and here I thought all this time that gays and lesbians were guys and girls. Sounds a bit redundant to me. "Chacun son gout" (to each his own) seems appropriate as I continue to remain neutral on this issue. Sometimes I'm just not smart enough to fully understand some things.

The reason this ad caught my eye today is because yesterday I rewrote an article (for part two of this book) which was published in the **FOR SINGLES ONLY** Magazine. It was called "Learning to Love Yourself". I had to revise the 7-year old column because I had to add the risk of AIDS to the more mundane, sexually transmitted diseases.

The ads continue to promise..."Meet the person of your dreams"..."They're waiting to meet you right now"...NY's hottest date lines"..."Talking personal ads of people who want to meet YOU" (huh?)..."Dr. Block's Therapeutic Fantasies" (telephone movies)..."Big Men*Small Men*All Men, Ah Men"...etc...

When someone jumps off the World Trade Center, he is not defying the law of gravity. He is confirming it! I also believe that when we break the natural laws...and we land in trouble, once again we are confirming the laws. I find this subject very painful and troublesome, but I cannot choose the ostrich approach just because it makes me "antsy" discussing it.

I have a dear friend who regularly advertises in the singles pages of our newspaper. I read his replies. I find a universal hunger permeating the letters he receives. They all want to fit the mold he has described, so that he will call them, and ease their loneliness. They repeat his ad almost verbatim, liking to do the same things he does. Some have replied to him several times over the course of three years. Still no Mr. Right for them.

The way to stop shopping in this "meat market" is not very difficult. Instead of looking for someone to love you, become a loving person to others. As you first develop self-love by ceasing to complain about your fat thighs, straggly or no hair (etc.) you will begin to magnetically bring into your life those who belong there. If you want a Robert Redford, you'd better look like Joan Collins. Otherwise, seek people at your own level, and stop dreaming of Ms. or Mr. Right. Otherwise, all of you dating will be done in your head. Remember, to be loved you must first become lovable.

# Seventy Seven

# Breastomania

This will probably become known as the "hardware bust caper". Just saw it on T.V. yesterday. This true story takes place in a small town in the U.S.A. The town hardware store is located right next to a Christian Books outlet.

Because of the continuing recession, the hardware store is ready to fold its tents and declare bankruptcy. Instead, the owner has a bright idea. Since his clerks' assets are in much better shape than his store's, he decides to show them off to his clientele. His clerks are two young, attractive and well-shaped blondes. He pays them $210 per six-hour day to display their "wares" in front of his customers, which now number in the *hundreds per day*! The clerks wear shoes, a G-string and a smile. Like many of the tools he sells, they are topless. So instead of the store going bust, the busts are keeping the store going.

I have always admired Yankee ingenuity, but nudity has been around since Adam and Eve. To sell tools through nudity is not ingenuity, but proof that the media has once again scored against what is decent and honorable. Sexploiting breastomania through the movies, magazines and videos degrades women and demeans those involved in encouraging it.

It would be interesting to see if business would continue to grow if they made the only exit from the store through the Christian Books outlet. If business would drop, it means that the men shopping in the hardware store are ashamed of what they are doing. If they are ashamed, then why shop there to begin with? Perhaps the bookstore can use a little ingenuity of its own. Have them dress up their clerks as Apostles, and greet customers as they enter the hardware store!

I know entrepreneurship made us a great nation, but do we have to make money at the expense of our fair sex? I think not! Check history; it will tell you that one of the first things to go when an empire falls is family unity and values. I am not happy that my 15-year *young* son and his peers know more and have seen more of the female anatomy than I did at twice his age. There is a time and a place for everything. Sexual maturity does not start in the 5th grade, yet girls are encouraged to wear lipstick and make-up before they are 12. This then puts pressure on the boys to perform "macho" acts...i.e., steal their parents' car and drive it, unlicensed...with predictable, dangerous results. Newsday reported at least five major accidents involving minors in the last few weeks on Long Island.

I suggest we let kids grow up as they do in school. Grade by Grade...Gradually! Don't push them into maturity before they are ready.

87

# Seventy Eight

# Mediation

Years ago a friend of mine, who knew of my interest in school children, suggested I join a mediation group working with other people of like interest. We were asked to volunteer our time to help solve minor problems dealing with kids interacting in harmful ways. I always worked with a woman for better balance. I did mediation for almost three years, and then decided to quit. Let me explain why.

One evening, my companion and I prepared to mediate another quarrel between two 5th grade girls, who went to the same school. It seems one of them had pushed the other off the school bus, an then threatened to beat her up if she ever boarded the same bus again. The principal suggested mediation rather than punishment at this time. A good idea you may agree, but let's follow the series of events a bit longer.

First, my associate and I were present. Also present was the head of mediation, who would type up the agreement once reached. Also, the parents of both girls were there. To top it off, the girls also had siblings at the meeting. Plus the janitor...who had to stay until we left the building. We had a total of *thirteen* people on hand, to mediate a push off a bus. It took us 2 1/2 hours to reach a favorable compromise. Imagine; 13 persons...eight of them adults, and five children, spending 2 1/2 hours to solve a simple problem.

I quit mediating after this case. Had the parents of the "slapper" slapped their own child five or six times when needed in the past, we would all have been home this particular evening. This was truly a case of parent neglect...neglecting to control th child when it was still possible. A few timely slaps on the buttocks, and it would never have become a 5th grade problem. I'm old fashioned enough to believe that to "spare the spank is to spoil the child". The spank must be given out of love, not anger or hatred. The child will understand, and learn there are laws that will have to be obeyed when older...and that home is the first school for learning.

If parents continue to be manipulated by their children, we will continue to waste valuable time on small matters. Give me a serious case again, an I'll make the time to be there and help mediate. Thirteen people times 2 1/2 hours equals 32 1/2 hours of time which could have been put to much better use.

I once gave a lecture in a public library entitled "How to Give Your Child A Healthy Self-Esteem!" Many people attended, but I feel only a few got the message I delivered. I aimed my entire talk at the parents there. I knew the kids' self-esteem would improve if I could help their parents' S.E. do the same, first!

# Seventy Nine

# P.O.M. Button

Buttons may be going out of vogue on clothing, but I now have my favorite button, which I expect to use for the rest of my life. This button does not go on clothes. Instead, it sits on my T.V. remote, mute. That's right...it's the mute button, and it's a most welcome one. Finally, a way to get rid of the loud, annoying commercials that use subliminal messages to make us want and need things most of us can do very well without.

Learning to love oneself includes developing the ability to know and differentiate between what we really want and what society demands we have in order to be accepted by our peers. This is especially true during the young formative years, when kids are so susceptible to the influence of their friends, who can destroy their fragile psyches by *rejecting* them from the group. I see kids wearing weird hairdos and clothes just to be accepted by other kids. Once again, this is the result of a poor self-image passed on from their parents.

Getting back to my mute, which allows me to get back at them (the infernal buy...buy...buy...messages) it has become my Armageddon button, which permits me to destroy the unwanted noise pollution. The P.O.M. which heads this vignette stands for Peace of Mind, a wonderful by-product of pushing the button when I want to. By the way, another way of fighting the T.V. "messages" (no longer called commercials...another Truth-in-Advertising lie) is not to buy the products lied and touted about. Peace of mind means the freedom to choose your purchases, based on your personal needs.

In order to feel good about yourself, you must make the final decision on how your monies will be spent. Self-esteem demands you satisfy the inner self...which will certainly add to your peace of mind.

Another happy button is the one on my telephone which cuts off unwanted recorded "messages"...also designed to sell you by seductive words. From my vantage point the button is alive and well, and would continue to thrive as we find more things to block out of our daily lives. On the mornings my garbage is picked up by the noisy truck, I wear two button-like devices in my ears, and continue to sleep through the racket. I also use these on flights. They eliminate the engine noises, as well as the occasional crying baby.

Button, button...who's got the button?

I do, and I'm glad I do. Go get your own buttons, and live your life with more peace of mind than you thought possible.

# Eighty

# Words

Read the word *"Love"* aloud...again...again! What does it bring to your mind. Anything? Or does it have to be tied to another word. Try *"Mom"*...Does this word automatically bring the word "Love" into focus? It does for me. Since my mother died 21 years ago, it also brings tears to my eyes. Here then is one word which can affect me both emotionally and physically. How about *"Hate"*! What does this one do for you? I have learned to hate the word "hate". I believe this word is learned more quickly by young children than the word "love". Children today love their jeans, tanktops, bikes, MacDonald's, CDs, rock stars, scary movies, and *tolerate* parents.

Conversely...these same kids can truly *hate* other kids, going to school, homework, vegetables, etc...My concern is how to turn hate into tolerance, since their neighborhood and school peers came from diverse backgrounds. One of my favorite words is *"Respect"*. My father taught me many years ago that I wold be respected to the exact degree that I would show respect to others.

Words can heal, hurt and even *kill* (study voodoo, and you'll see how words can kill). We know laughter can heal, and laughter is the direct result of hearing a string of words delivered on purpose for a mirthful effect. We know words used by parents can humiliate and destroy self-esteem...the most important singular trait needed for successful living. When we say to them, "You're stupid!" or "I hate you!"..."I wish you were never born!", we are in effect, destroying the good image they are trying hard to build up and maintain for their emotional and psychological survival and well-being.

Give your kid a test, unknown to him. Count the times he says *hate* and the times he says *love* for one week. The ratio of hate vs. love will astonish you. Here is what Epictetus wrote about this (circa 50-120): "Whatever you would make habitual, practice it; and if you would not make a thing habitual, do not practice it, but accustom yourself to something else". Once again, the wisdom of Ancient Greece paves the way for better intentions.

Keep a list and show your child his lopsided hate/love connection, and let him/her know how this will affect his/her entire life. It is when words become permanent labels that the damage becomes great. Kikes, micks, guineas, niggers...when these words are used by anyone, it shows what a low self-esteem the speaker has. A wise person once said that there are two types of people living on Earth. Those living in the gutter, and those on the sidewalk. There is a constant battle going on between these two groups. The gutter people try to drag the sidewalkers into the gutter with them. Sidewalk people want to pull the gutterites up to join them above, where the view of the world is much *cleaner!*

90

# Eighty One

# Insanity

I saw another bumper sticker earlier today. It said, "Insanity is inherited. You get it from your kids!" Clever, but untrue. The fact is, all your kids can do is to dredge up *your* days as a teenager, and *your* insanities at the time. But you choose to conveniently forget that you too drove your parents "off the wall" during the hormone-disturbed years. I'm quite sure I personally aggravated my folks during my **know-it-all** period, when they miraculously became old-fashioned overnight, and their life experiences worthless to me.

As you well know, what goes around comes around, and now it's my turn to be old-fashioned, and my teenager misunderstood. Oh well, as the inscription inside King Solomon's gold ring read: "This too shall pass!" As a stepfather, my options in rearing him are limited. Fortunately, he has a more modern "mom" with whom daily communication is easier. Sometimes it's through her that I find out what's on his mind.

When I do motivational counseling with parents, I find that most of them carry the burden of guilt on their tired shoulders. I say tired because nothing can weigh a person down more than feelings of guilt, which are cumulative. Guilt is truly an old-fashioned idea, used primarily to control people...as religious institutions love to do.

I believe that guilt should be felt only if we decide to continue actions which we *know* are harmful to someone else, whether it be a person or an animal, such as a pet. Otherwise, if we feel guilty over past events, we might as well include feeling guilty over the way the American Indian was mistreated over three centuries ago. After all, where does it all end?

It ends when a commitment is made to immediately stop doing what hurts others; then guilt simply melts away into the past, where it began and where it now belongs.

Guilt is old-fashioned...parents not necessarily. I will not use guilt to control anyone's behavior, including mine. Using it as a punitive weapon is a lose-lose proposition, since both self-images involved suffer negatively.

Whenever I use guilt to control or punish...I feel guilty! Hence, I just don't do it. And a great psychological load has been lifted from my shoulders, and allows me to use a faster pace in my quest for certain goals...both personal and financial.

I'd like to see a new bumper sticker in front of me when I drive. Let it simply say: *"Guilt Sucks!"*

"Go, and hurt no more" is probably the best advice to give to those who want to lead guiltless lives.

# Eighty Two.

# Happiness

Today is the best day of the rest of your life. Live in the now. Don't live in the past or in the future. The present requires your full attention! A study conducted by the Sociology Department at Duke University on the concept of "peace of mind" came to the conclusion that much unhappiness is caused by our unwholesome preoccupation with past failures and mistakes. Further studies have shown that we spend 60% of our awake time thinking of the past; 20% is spent on the future and only 20% on the present, which is the only time we have any control over. We are so engrossed in the *me*s of our life we forget there are others out there living in their past *me*s as well. If it's axiomatic that we are what we think about then it's up to us to change our thinking, thus changing the very fabric of our lives.

If we flip the big ☐Me☐ over...

it becomes........... ☐We☐ ...and We can do much more together than Me and Me separately. In union there is strength!

Happiness does not come all at once, as in an explosion. Rather, happiness comes in bits and pieces; sometimes it sneaks up subliminally, when you are totally unaware of it. This can happen when your mind is on some negative aspect of your life. Suddenly, you realize you have been listening to one of your best-loved pieces of music, coming from an external source. Your mood changes immediately, as it now conforms to the new and more powerful stimulus. Gone for awhile is your negativity, as it has now been replaced with a "happy" memory through a process of "mind-changing". Thus, the good news is that we can change our minds anytime we want. However, we must choose to do so. To put this another way, we can choose to be happy anytime we want. All it takes is a mental decision. For an experiment, try telling someone bad news while you are smiling. It is virtually impossible to do this, since smiling automatically changes our thinking from negative to positive. I've used this test in over 90 different cities at my seminars. No one has ever told bad news properly when smiling. The great William James once said: "In order to become enthusiastic, you must act enthusiastically!" Act happily, and your mind will come up with the reasons for being happy. Beats negative thinking any day.

The greatest happiness comes as a result of doing for others, for this means more than one person is involved in this powerful emotional high. My Webster's Ninth New Collegiate Dictionary defines happiness as "a state of well-being and contentment". A wonderful state-ment, I feel!

Happiness is following an adage of the great Greek philosopher

Empedocles (490-430 B.C.), who advised us thusly: "We would have inner peace, but will not look within!" Happiness to me is also when a waitress asks me how the food is, and my mouth is not full at the time, and I can actually answer. Happiness is watching major life changes take place when I work with people as a motivational therapist. Happiness is listening to a great classic work, composed centuries ago, and yet, as fresh as today's headlines. Happiness is seeing my son's report card filled with A's.

Happiness is accepting yourself as you are, subject to changes only you decide upon. Working on becoming a better you will take up so much of your time you will not have any left to change others, which is as God intended it to be.

*Trying to make things easy results in great difficulties*
Chinese Proverb

# Eighty Three

# Carpe Diem

This Latin phrase meaning "seize the day" is now being spotted all over the country. It's being replicated on T-shirts, on coffee mugs, ties, bumper stickers and other paraphernalia. It's the in thing to say...yet to most of us it will remain just that; i.e. a thing to say or show. What we don't know is that this is only a partial quote from Horace, who lived from 65 to 8 B.C. His full quote bears repeating...because it puts the emphasis on the first part by explaining it.

"Carpe Diem, Quam Minimum Credula Postero" meaning "seize the day, put no trust in the morrow". I believe Horace meant that it's OK to plan for tomorrow but don't count on it to necessarily happen as you plan. His concern, as yours should be was to live fully today, for there are no guarantees beyond now. If the great artists and authors of the world worried about tomorrow very little would have been accomplished.

Many examples abound. Goethe, writing for 40 years finished FAUST at **82**. Titian painted BATTLE OF LEPANTS when he was **98**. Michelangelo finished painting the ceiling of the Sistine Chapel lying on his back on a scaffold when he was almost **90**. At age **83** Tennyson wrote CROSSING THE BAR. Churchill and Grandma Moses began to paint when in their 80s. And the list goes on and on. According to research 2/3 of all the great works in the world were done by people past age 60. Do you think these authors, artists, musicians and sculptors worried about tomorrow? If they did none of them would have begun their greatest accomplishments, and the world of art and culture would be far poorer as a result.

If you get an idea worth doing, forget time frames. Time was invented by man to serve him...and not be a slave to. What do Arnold Schwarzenegger, Lou Ferrigno and Jacques Weisel have in common? All three of us have exactly the same number of muscles. However, two of us chose to exercise them to full potential. This was done on a daily basis, with no worry about what the next day might bring. The end results for them are the awards and accolades they have been receiving since they first began. Although I exercise almost daily I chose mental commitments related to my career. I do my work daily...hoping but not necessarily counting on my tomorrows. Happiness does not come to anyone; it just is. Since life is but a journey and not a destination, it is wise to put up milestones along the way...so that we know how far we've come. But just as we cannot put up milestones for the miles we haven't covered yet, so should we not worry over the days we have not lived yet. Better to have an overall plan for the future, and concentrate on doing what makes you happy now, for there may not be a future in your future.

# Eighty Four

# NEWS

Newspaper headline: Today 14,532 planes flew to different cities in the United States; not a single fatality was reported. Or: The National Safety Council reports no deaths on the roads this past Thanksgiving holiday. A final headline in your local newspaper might read: There were no accidents on the major highways during the morning and evening rush-hours.

How long would these headlines hold your attention? Probably just long enough to *read them*...before you skip to some *juicier bit* of news--filled with blood and guts and murder and mayhem. I make it my business to read the comics first so that my mental outlook is positive...since we all know that laughter heals. Then I read *headlines* to know what's going on...and fully skip the gore which makes up most of the articles.

This past weekend Newsday published a 32 page supplement commemorating th 50th anniversary of the bombing of Pearl Harbor. It would take several hours to read, and would be a reminder to many of us of the *awfulness* of war. The articles would certainly stir up old angers in millions of people who were involved directly or indirectly during World War II. A rather unpleasant way to spend the Thanksgiving weekend.

"As a man thinketh in his heart" means how he/she *feels*, since there is no record of the actual feeling word in the Bible. Emotional writing excites us and leads to irrational behavior if it is of a negative nature. It also causes ulcers, heart attacks, shingles, headaches and a myriad of other psychosomatically induced illnesses. Why punish our bodies by reliving the "angst" we may have suffered many years ago? We then become the losers since most of those responsible for our anguish are now dead or dying, being at least 68 years old. (18 when inducted in the Japanese army plus 50 years).

I believe remembering our lost ones is important if we can keep outdated hatred out of our thoughts. Otherwise we will continue to perpetuate the separation and alienation of the world's different races and religions-- and never reach the goal of the United Nations, i.e. peace on earth. Because of religious persecution I spent my 8th birthday running from the Nazis. My 9th and 10th birthdays were not much better...spent as a refugee in North Africa with little food or clothing. Understandably I did not grow much during these 3 years of physical and mental (no school) deprivation.

As I see it...*a pessimist is one who is always looking forward to the past! Honor the past*...but don't spend too much time in it. Those of us who believe in "the good old days" are generally suffering from a poor memory. Please check yours.

# *Eighty Five*

# Wed-Dog License

The following may be a fable, and then again it may not be. Depends on your point of reference. This is what I believe, based on what I see.

There once was a man on line in City Hall. Behind him was a couple, obviously much in love since they seemed attached at the hip. Both the man and the couple were waiting for licenses...the first for his dog and the latter to make their bliss official. The City Hall clerk had other things on his mind, and absentmindedly had the dog-lover fill out the marriage license and vice-versa with the moonstruck boy and girl.

Thusly it came to pass that the dog license is now renewable each year and the marriage license is for life. The opposite, which was originally the intent made more sense but mankind has been paying the price of one clerk's blunder ever since. The idea of the licenses was this: a dog license is for life, since most people keep a dog until "death do them part". The marriage license was to be renewed each year, thus guaranteeing that the couple would continue to work on the marriage so that their license would not be revoked on their anniversary date. Licenses for marriage should read *until divorce/death do us part* since over 50% will end in divorce.

The annual renewable marriage license makes even more sense than ever. It would eliminate billions of dollars turned over to landsharks who "settle" the remnants of painful divorces, from an adversarial position. Another idea would be to give only checks as wedding presents postdated 5 years ahead. If the couple stayed together that long it meant they had earned the right to use the gifts. If they split you could always re-use the uncashed check for the next wedding, and so on. In the long run you'd probably save a lot of money. You could then use some of it to give larger presents at confirmations, bar-mitzvahs and bas-mitzvahs.

Which brings me to my final idea on the subject. Since by Jewish law a boy becomes a man at 13, why not have him marry at the same time and save a bundle. I went to one last year which cost more than most first weddings. This bar-mitzvah did include the proverbial kitchen sink...and then some. I kept waiting for a bride to show up but had to be satisfied with a single celebration. At least the boy did get to cash the checks. He earned the right to keep the money by fulfilling his obligation to learn the meaning of manhood. Let's hope what he learned stays with him longer than the money will.

Today I believe too many kids fall in lust and then marry. Only after they truly love themselves can they *fall in love* with another.

# Eighty Six

# 2B or not 2B

"To be or not to be"...That *is* the question.

First asked by Hamlet as written by Shakespeare this question now takes on more significance than ever before. In order to understand its current importance I'd like to suggest an alternate question for you to answer. It's simply this: ask yourself "Who am I?" Do you answer with one of the following? (a) I'm just a sales clerk; (b) I'm only a housewife; (c) I'm simply the janitor; (d) I'm merely the bookkeeper; (e) I'm but a small fish in a big pond; (f) My job is hardly worth talking about; (g) I'm nothing more than a glorified office clerk.

If one of the above describes your self-appraisal, you will continue to be what you have accepted as your self-image. It means you have decided to go through life working mostly from a faulty consciousness. Your talents are not coordinated with your capacities, resulting in an "average" life...usually as a victim of circumstances.

When we study the lives of people like Albert Einstein...who failed math while in school, we find that all great achievers are inner-driven. The will to win or excel is a result of innate intelligence pushing out to new horizons. According to Einstein he only had two original ideas, and they were the direct products of his reason (left brain) plus *intuition* (right brain).

Saying that you are only such and such means you are giving up your birthright as God's most important creation, with what science now calls *unlimited potential!*

Going through life without tapping our subconscious for its immeasurable wealth is like going through life as a pauper with a never touched bankbook having a balance of $100,000,000.

I become truly disturbed when I meet people who are carbon copies of people who are carbon copies of people ...ad *nauseum.*

Instead of thinking the good life is impossible look at the word impossible in a more imaginative fashion, and see it as *I.M. Possible.* To feel that way one must begin to think for oneself. I may not agree "in toto" with Henry David Thoreau when he wrote: "I have lived some 30 years on this planet, and I have yet to hear the first syllable of valuable or even earnest advice from my seniors". I believe the advice you get from within is far more accurate if it is a result of a gut feeling, i.e. intuition.

# Eighty Seven

# Self Love

Did you hug yourself today? Yup, I do mean yourself. Because if you don't psychologically hug yourself daily...the hugging of anyone else becomes meaningless. Let me explain. Great-grandparents with a low self-esteem will beget grandparents with a low self-esteem, who will beget parents with a low self-esteem. They in turn will continue the pattern and beget children with a low self-esteem, who will then give you grandchildren with the same low self-esteem, and so on into infinity.

For an example of the above concept at work, did you ever watch a family of three generations "waddle" past you? Doctors tell us that less than 1% of "fatties" suffer from metabolic or thyroid disorders. The other 99% "overweights" are self-constructed.

In his classic work "Reality Therapy" Dr. William Glasser says that we all have the same two basic human needs: the need to *love and be loved*, and to feel *worthwhile* to ourself and others. Our health and happiness depend on our receiving huge doses of both on a regular basis.

On the proverbial scale of 0 to 10 where do you register on the love-loving meter? Using a measuring spoon marked self-worth (soup size) do you fill it or barely wet it with a drop? Life will deliver to you exactly what your mind thinks about all day long. When you're finally ready to face reality sit down and try to recall what went on in your mind in the past 12 hours. If you like what you discovered about yourself and your thoughts stay with them. If you don't...change them!

A good way to begin a change for the better is to follow Robert Ingersoll's sage advice. He said: My creed is this: *happiness* is the only good. The place to be happy is here. The time to be happy is now. The way to be happy is to *make others so!*" I believe his message is self-fulfilling.

A recent local newspaper had a roving reporter interview a group of people aged 8 to 70. She only asked them one question: "What do you want to be when you grow up?" Here are the answers: "...I would like to be a playboy like Dudley Moore in "Arthur"...independently rich singer...sex object...two feet taller...20 pounds lighter...a famous ballroom dancer...grow up to be an old lady with class..." the elder statesman said: "you should have asked me that 70 years ago." Finally, the youngest answered: *"I want to be a nurse and help people when they get sick."* Wow! The only mature, humane "want" came from an 8 year old. Everyone else was part of the "gimme, gimme" philosophy. A sad commentary on our once role-model nation, and a great vote for hope in the next generation.

This is one 8-year old who can definitely hug herself because she is both loving and loved. I would also bet that had she been in Brooklyn yesterday and partaken in the scramble by 100 people for $50,000 dropped in the street by a thief, she would have returned the money she picked up. (The other 100 people, to my disgust but not surprise, did not). As for the group being surveyed, they do not *really* want what they said to the reporter. After all, didn't the great author Napoleon Hill teach us that: "Whatever the mind of man/woman can *conceive and believe*, man can *achieve!*"

Last week was Thanksgiving, and I'd like to voice my thanks for a fine past year. First, I'm thankful for my continued personal growth, as I exchange ideas with people from all walks of life through my lectures, seminars, TV show and this column. I'm sure that I've learned much more from them than I have taught. I'm thankful for an America where I can state my opinions freely, without fear of censorship or reprisal. I'm grateful for my friends and peers, but I'm also very saddened to know that fully one-third of all that has been cooked for Thanksgiving in America will end up in garbage cans. When we were refugees of WW2 in North Africa our family of four lived on less per *week* than what the average home here threw out on this holiday. So be grateful, and quit your bellyachin' cause we never had it so good. Eat the turkey, and don't become one! Harken to H.D. Thoreau's wisdom: "A man is rich in proportion to the number of things he can afford to let alone!"

*Your peers won't care how much you know*
*until they know how much you care*

Anonymous

99

# *Eighty Eight*

# Dr. Jacques

Having given myself a doctorate in Positive Living I would like at this time to share a prescription I wrote for myself, or anyone who wants to succeed at living. The formula is designed to cure "mental botulism"...a disease which affects 95% of our total adult population. It consists of a hefty dose of *mega-vitamins*, or as I have renamed them Posimins. (Positive Vitamins)

Here's how my system works. You take my Posimins for 30 days 3 times per day and then...stand back and watch your life change forever. These vitamins may be taken orally, wherein a tutor is available to you at any time, day or night. Or you can take them physically by reading books or listening to tapes on a daily basis. The dosage to be used works this way: 3 units of Vitamin A, one for Attitude, the second for Acceptance and the third for Aptitude. Your Attitude unit will guarantee a positive outlook toward everything in your life. Your Aptitude unit will help increase your money-making skills. Finally, your Action unit will get you started today! Whether you take your daily doses orally or physically, they must eventually be internalized...as a permanent addition to your subconscious.

Vitamin B is for Belief. The belief that you are a unique human being, capable of *anything* you really want. Belief will enable you to unleash much of your unused potential, so that you are no longer part of the "average" majority.

Take three units of Vitamin C and you'll never be left out in the cold. One unit is for Caring...a very valuable quality, which you must increase in your daily contact with others. One unit for Confidence, which will grow in huge quantities as you continue to take your supplements. The third unit of vitamin C is for Commitment...to life and truly living it!

The D Vitamin will bring sunshine in your life as you increase your Desire for happiness (1 unit) and renew your Dedication to help others improve theirs. (Also 1 unit).

Vitamin E will improve your sex life, since it stands for Enthusiasm. Need I say more?

The single unit of Vitamin F will make you Fearless, and eager to face each day's challenges as opportunities for personal growth.

Two units of Vitamin G are required. One is for Goals, which need no explanation. The other is for God. Believing in a Superior Intelligence shows yours to be intelligent as well. Also, if life is to be Good for you...and you take God away from Good, all you have left is a big 0 for *nothing!* Interesting, isn't it?

Vitamin H, used in 2 units represents Health and Habits. They're tightly interwoven; eliminate the bad habits and watch your health improve. *Immediately!*

Vitamin I is for Imagination, which is your ability to create your own images-in-action. A very Important gift...important standing for the second I. *Make people feel important!* They will then make your "I am" feel important as well.

Taking all 9 vitamins daily will synergistically blend them all, and turn them into Vitamin J...for Joy of living! And isn't this where I came in?

By the way, this Mega-Vitamin plan only works if you do. After all let's remember that life gives you *nothing*, except the opportunity to create your own destiny. Life brings you nothing and takes you nowhere. To find out which vitamins you need more of, examine your attitudes and lifestyle today! If they need change begin at once.

Remember what Ovid (43B.C.-18A.D.) told us: "Nothing endures but change". Attend seminars, read books and listen to tapes which will *reinforce* the person you want to be. Forget all media; they only stress (double-meaning) the negative side of life. The only place for negatives is a photographer's darkroom.

Become more flexible with your daily activities. Don't get bogged down in the same old rut (a coffin with the ends kicked out)...and learn to laugh! It saved Norman Cousins' life more than once. We read in Proverbs 14:13..."in laughter the pain of heart is eased". One very important point. *Laugh at yourself* most of the time. Don't take yourself too seriously. After all, no one else does. To top it all, you know you'll never leave this world alive.

If you still don't Believe (vitamin B) that you can become anything you set your mind to, follow the advice of Mahatma Ghandi. He admonished us thusly: "Men often become what they believe themselves to be. If I believe I cannot do something it makes me incapable of doing it. But when I believe I can, then I acquire the ability to do it, even if I didn't have it at the beginning."

*Believe in yourself. I believe in you!*

# Eighty Nine

# Mother's Day!

I'd like to ban Mother's Day forever!...that's right, I did say ban! I'm not looking for trouble.  The point is, I'd like to switch it to a Happy Mother's Year!  The way I see it, if mom deserves honoring it shouldn't be once per year.  It should be done consistently...all the time.  I know the retailers love this day (created it) but wouldn't they rather enjoy a full year of sales related to moms?  This annual ritual of hypocrisy has come to mean that we can take her for granted the rest of the time.  As long as we pay homage to her once a year.

As a nation we're famous for making holidays out of anything we can make a buck at.  This morning at a local restaurant I watched the faces of those engaged in the ritual of "Love for a Day!"  Not too many happy ones; this from both sides of the relationship.  Kids and husbands who browbeat and abuse mom all year-round go through the motions demanded by society.  Mothers who tyrannize their offsprings (and husbands) now await their annual homage.  Plus the gifts!  How about the syrupy cards, written by professional writers...with meaningless messages much of the time.  This isn't a show of love!  No one benefits from this type of holiday.  Even the retailers would be better off if moms were honored regularly.  With *appropriate* gifts.

Instead, what do stores recommend you buy on this day?  Toasters, can openers, irons, coffee makers, waffle irons, sets of silverware and dishes, ad nauseum...all designed to keep her in the *kitchen*, working.  A great way to prove love on this occasion.

When you think about it most of us cannot afford a mom.  If we had to pay her for all she does.  Consider an average day: she's a cook, laundress, chauffeur, gardener, psychologist, lover, family doctor, dietician, etc...plus a full-time job outside her home.  Even paying minimum wage would wreck most men's paychecks.

As children we cannot afford to take mothers for granted any longer.  She does not need an *annual bribe*.  Our actions all year round will show what we think of her.

As husbands our respect and continued consideration for her will show her how we feel.

Here's another idea.  We could establish a National Drug Day!  This is to help celebrate the huge sales of pain-killers and drugs sold to moms, so that they can daily cope with motherhood.  I personally know quite a few mothers who cannot function without their daily Valium or Lithium...not counting the millions of aspirins they take daily.  The medical professional now admits that much of this pill-popping is due to stress and frustration...brought on by the family unit. Over 50% of the world goes to bed nightly hungry for food. Over 95% of Americans go to bed nightly hungry for recognition! Which is free!

Make Mom feel important, needed, and loved...and you can skip the annual ritual, played badly in front of a very disinterested party. And Mom, please remember your responsibilities to the next generation. You do have to earn the respect of your family. As prophet Ezekiel once said: "as is the mother, so is her daughter (son)." Also, remember that *becoming* a mother may be difficult...but *being* one is crucial!

*Despise not thy mother when she is old*
Proverbs 23:22

# Ninety

# 8 Power Words

"It is done unto you as you believe" is one of the most powerful phrases ever uttered by the sage from Bethlehem. Modern-day psychologists are beginning to see and accept the meaning of this ancient wisdom. Religious leaders have always known about it, but have not stressed its value and importance so that it becomes a way of life for us. Perhaps a full understanding of this universal law would take away too much power from the clergy. Ergo they suppress its ability to influence us because there would be less need for their services if we truly internalized this pearl of wisdom.

Even the medical profession knows and appreciates its value in the healing arts. Placebos (sugar pills) have been around for many years and work on 30-60% of the people they are given to. It is only the *belief* in the pill which causes the positive results, and not the sugary pills themselves. Once again the power comes directly from within us; those who study the human mind call it the self-fulfilling prophecy. Its potency is proven daily in the business world as well as in our private lives. For example, we know that sales reps subconsciously create the condition they expect to happen...and then are not surprised to find it happened as they "predicted". Thirty years ago, when I truly *believed* that every home should have its own educational tools I won the International Sales Award from a very prestigious 200-year old company which I believed had the best products available. Later in my sales career when I sold for $ and not out of product belief, I paid my bills but did not excel in 3 other companies until I went back to products I honestly believed in. (The reason I believed in encyclopedias for the home is that as refugees in North Africa my brother and I were not allowed to go to the French schools for the three years we spent there).

The same concept holds true in all personal relationships. If you believe you will be turned down for a date, you will create the conditions (subliminally) for a negative answer. Go for a job and believe you won't get it, and you'll be right all the time.

Since belief and faith are often used interchangeably it behooves us to examine our level of faith when we want something to happen. If our faith is strong, we will generally prevail. If it is weak or unstable, it will help defeat our purpose. Since faith presupposes a strong belief and loyalty in a Creator, this is where our wants and needs should begin to manifest. If what you want is noble and benefits many, and you truly feel you *deserve* it, it should self-fulfill!

# Ninety One

# How's Your P.C.?

I'm not referring to your personal computer, but rather to your Prosperity Consciousness, which comes from your *personal computer*...(a.k.a. the brain). It is a well-known fact that people almost always earn within 10% above or below their image of themselves, and that the way to increase earnings is to improve their self-esteem. It is incredible to me that in this age of continuing scientific discoveries most of us still harbor a low self-esteem, which translates into low to average earnings for most of our lives. Dr. Paul Brand, world-renowned surgeon claims that as I write this vignette, 5,000,000,000,000,(5 trillion) chemical operations are occurring in my brain...per second! Without traffic jams interfering with my thoughts. He also says that every one of the 100 trillion cells in the human body has continuing access to the brain. Further and newer research shows that *each* one of these numerous cells has its own intelligence, and that communication exists between them and the brain. Given these few facts on the magnificent creation we call our body, how can we in good conscience walk around with a low self-image?

Unfortunately, the blame can be put directly to our personal mental computer...which absorbs negative input as readily as we feed it, with disastrous results. Since the subconscious is nonjudgmental it believes everything stored in it, thus reinforcing our deepest feelings of inadequacy. Perhaps our PC should be told about the most miraculous engine ever invented. Weighing in at less than a pound, with a life expectancy of 80 years, this 1 horsepower engine processes over 2,000 gallons of fluids per day. Each valve in this engine operates an average of 4,500 times per hour, and will have run through 2.5 billion cycles before it is retired for good. The engine is called the *human heart*, and it comes free with every body. I wonder what it would cost to reproduce it with all its incredible qualities? As a pump it pushes blood through 70,000 miles of blood vessels, traveling over 168,000,000 miles daily!

I believe it's time our personal computer re-evaluated itself, exchanging the negative messages it carries around for new and positive affirmations. We were not given the most miraculous brain and body to match to waste them in a lifetime of self-pity.

We were meant to soar as the "altus", mythical Greek bird which could fly higher and deeper than all others. Not to grovel with a "victim...everything happens to me" mentality. We were all born to win; many of us proceeded to become failures at life, or average. Average is a mid-point between the best and the worst. We can choose greatness, just as we once chose mediocrity. It only takes a moment to turn the switch on our *personal* computer.

# Ninety Two.

# G.O.D.

Those are the letters on several trucks I see being driven on Long Island highways. No, they don't stand for GOD...rather an acronym for Guaranteed Overnight Delivery. Even God can't match that speed. I know, because many people pray to God daily and hope for instant delivery from problems. Usually they are very disappointed and lay full blame on their Creator. This is a result of misunderstanding the God concept. Many people still cling to the old idea that their god is in charge of the world's largest supermarket, and will deliver the goods upon request. The goods include material things, health, spouses, children, and whatever else the human mind can conjure up to receive.

What is not understood too well is that once the universal laws came into being, *no one*, including the gods we worship could change them. Not overnight, not in several days, weeks, months, years, centuries of even millenia. Many years ago I saw a French movie with the great comedian Fernandel. It was called "La loi c'est la loi!" meaning "the law is the law!" I don't remember the movie but the title still holds. The trick then is to learn the Law, and how to use it. To follow the law is to consistently "hit the mark", and to sin is to "miss the mark"...thus breaking the law and inviting unwelcome consequences. I find my life runs much more smoothly when I let the Universe run itself, without any interference from me. As a matter of fact the less my thinking brain does its "stuff" the more feeling my life becomes...hence more enriched. It then becomes much easier to follow Shakespeare and his dictum: "This above all: to thine own self be true. And it must follow as the night the day, Thou canst not then be false to any man."

Perhaps the old joke holds more meaning than I gave it credit. It goes like this: "when a person falls in love with himself it's the beginning of a lifelong romance." Leo Buscaglia has his special "I love Leo" time, when he nurtures his self-esteem. Yet nobody in modern times has given more love away to others. It's a well known fact that we cannot give to others what we don't possess. Love yourself (not Narcissism) and let it spill over into your outside life and relationships. This will benefit both you and the recipients of your positive feelings.

"Love conquers all" is not a platitude; it is the law of the universe. In holistic health it is recognized as the greatest healing force we can muster up against catastrophic illnesses. Since most physical problems begin as a disease of the mind, we can begin to work on changing our inner selves, through the development of strong, loving and ethical codes of behavior. Good health will follow, leaving illness in a permanent vacuum.

# Ninety Three

# Options From Within

As the title of my book implies I truly and fully believe that our eventual happiness will be a result of inner choices, not based on learning or conditioning from without. Dr. Theodore Reik once wrote an excellent book on psychology called "Listening with the third ear." This is exactly what I am suggesting. We must learn to listen to the insightful, intuitive ideas that seem to come out of "nowhere" when we least expect them. These are the options I am referring to in my title. The problem is this; if we don't use them as they occur, they don't come back.

Reminds me of the time Opportunity knocked on this man's door, and he couldn't answer because he was too busy in his backyard...looking for a four-leaf clover. The idea is to stay inside of yourself when looking for answers, and keep external noises at bay. This can be likened to a meditative state, wherein the thinking brain is asleep and our feeling side wide awake. This enables us to tap into the universal mind and draw from it the wisdom of the ages. Besides intuition, this is also known as "gut feeling" or hunch. Whatever the name...use it or lose it.

Most people go through life driving in "neutral" because they have little or no trust in their innate potential. Instead of planning goals for big results they are content to accept goals straight out of a box of trivia. The winners choose their goals; all others settle for them. They believe that this is what the Creator wants for them...mediocrity! Since there is no real purpose in mediocrity, life becomes dull, slow and meaningless. And then we die.

Instead, if we decided to define, outline and plan a life shored up by a strong *purpose*, a reason for living...there is no telling how much more of our untapped potential we could reach. If the purposeful goal outlives us, so much the better. Goals are thoughts materialized; purpose is a feeling which goes on and on, and can be passed on after us. Generally, it is closely tied to universal values and therefore transcends us as individuals.

The first step to developing a purpose (vs. goals) is to follow the advice found in two of the most powerful words ever put together. They were carved over the entrance to the Delphic oracle in Greece, and their wisdom is timeless: *"Know Thyself!"*

The second step is to "change thyself", based on what you find out about the real, inner you. We all agree this is easier said than done, but repetition brings recognition. And persistence will bring permanent results.

The third step is the toughest of all. It is one of omission, not commission. It can be put into four simple words: *"Do not change others!"* Just become an example to others.

# Dead Right

"He who seeks revenge should dig two graves" is a very wise old Chinese warning. Couples with negative terms such as *"to hold* a grudge"..."*carry* guilt around"..."*loaded* down with worries"..."*running* around scared"..."*walking* a tightrope"..."*lugging* hatred around"..."*nurturing* hatred"..."*nursing* anger", they all imply some physical activity on the part of the person thinking these thoughts. Physical activity is tiring, as is mental activity which depicts bodily actions. As conditioned beings we drain our life-force whenever we think in negative pictures or metaphors. Unfortunately this takes up most of our waking time. The result is that many times we would rather be "dead right" (when our ego is on the line) than alive and healthy.

Ego is defined as "the self, especially when contrasted with another self" in my lexicon. Since this self is made up of millions of imprints put on us by others while growing up, it stands to reason that the resultant "self" is not really who we are but what we have become. Who we are lies buried under an avalanche of negative data. Psychologists tell us that the average 5 year old child has been programmed with over 15,000 reasons not to feel good about himself/herself. As these mini-digs at our psyche add up, they form a formidable wall behind which we hide our true selves.

Since the best defense is known to be a strong offense, we quickly resort to maintaining our fragile egos by attacking others. Thus the phrase "dead right", since attacking others puts strain and stress on our emotional security. Hence, illness and death at younger ages than ever before, as we cope with life in a self-destructive manner.

The answer of course lies in restructuring our damaged egos. The best ways include using positive affirmations, learning to truly forgive others and ourselves, developing an altruistic philosophy wherein we give of ourselves through "pro bono" time. You'll notice that we are mixing things to do for ourselves as well as for others; this will help to balance our lives by helping both our inner and outer selves. Peace of mind is the final result; no one has ever died from too much peace of mind. I believe this is your ultimate goal in life, as it is mine.

Digging into the negative past is good *only* if it results in discarding the "old garbage" stored therein. Review it once, keep the good past and forget the rest. Concentrate on the now, which is the only time we can control. Stop listening to your mind, and begin to hear what's in your *heart*. Jess Laird, Ph.D. advises us to work in 15-minute segments in our lives and watch it work like a charm. Not a bad idea for good mental health.

# Ninety Five

# Puppy Love

My mother was brought up in a very orthodox Jewish home in Czechoslovakia. Her mother wore a traditional wig and her father never shaved. He grew a beard, and he never trimmed it. My mother was brought up to believe all animals were "untouchable", except for ritual slaughter and then cooking. When I first brought my newly-purchased Chinese pug to her home she recoiled in horror, thinking the dog (Frisky) was part of the rat family, only larger and uglier. But Frisky had other ideas. She knew she was born with a definite purpose in mind, which she proceeded to unravel.

Frisky was the most lovable living being I had ever run across, and she earned her name by being the most playful pet (I hate that word) ever to live with me. She knew the real meaning of *unconditional* love. I wish I had learned that lesson from her many years ago. It would have spared me much anguish in life.

Anyhow, it did not take long for Frisky to worm her way (no pun intended) into my mother's heart. Frisky was the first living animal (aside from chickens and ducks) my mom ever touched...because she was *touched* by something which gave love with no rhyme or reason whatsoever.

Mom came from the old fashioned school that says affection and love are not displayed openly. My father followed suit and showed little of his love and affection for my brother and me. But we knew we were loved. They escaped with us from Brussels to Casablanca in 1940, where they often fed us from their own paltry rations. When I was 19, I fractured my left femur and ended up in the hospital, tied down with weights in my bed. My father turned white as a sheet and almost fainted when he first saw me. Another time...when I told my father of my impending divorce (at age 39) he said to me, for what I believe was the first time: "Son, I love you!" And my tough old dad cried for me.

Getting back to Frisky, she touched many lives with her playful, loving personality. If I believed I could be reincarnated as an animal I would choose a life like Frisky's for my next sojourn on earth. Without a care in the world she touched all the people she met, just as a bee would pollinate the flowers it landed on.

Perhaps some animals are closer to the source of life than humans are. It is our job to learn from them what they have to teach us. Love keeps us alive longer, too. Frisky lived to be 15, then had to be put away because she was losing control of her major faculties. I hope I can develop this incredible "joi de vivre" which she had. I'm sure she's in dog-heaven, teaching them to love *unconditionally,* no matter how badly their next owners might treat them! And in China, they actually *eat* dogs!!!

# Ninety Six

# Brainwashing

Today, if you're average you'll use up 57,600 seconds while being awake. During these seconds you'll be bombarded by 18,000 different messages. This comes out to one message every 3.2 seconds you spend awake. Much of that will come from advertising. Although the United States has only 6% of the world population, it produces 57% of the total global advertising for local consumption. I'm glad I don't have to shop in supermarkets, since I'd have to decide on my purchases from shelves loaded down with over 24,000 separate products. Mindboggling, to say the least.

And this is just the beginning, futurists tell us. For example, there have been more changes in the last 20 years than in the past 200, according to the experts. And futurists also tell us that the year 2001 will be as different for us as we are to the 1890s. And yet...there is some hope for us. To quote a great Frenchman, Alphonse Karr: "The more things change, the more they remain the same." He understood over a century ago that although the outer trappings may change, people will always be people. And it's up to people to manage change. We cannot delegate this to science, since change comes from within and science deals with the outside person. I believe that to manage change we must remain in full self-control. The more the changes on the *outside*, the more strength is required to *remain the same inside*.

Too many American feel frightened and helpless because they have lost control of the problems brought about by our current society. They are easily *dis-stressed* by new (not improved) pressures on their lives, and they've become highly cynical about most things they read in the daily papers or see on television. Perhaps what we need are less futurists and more presentists, people who can deal with what's happening now...and work on it!

It's far easier to look into a crystal ball and predict the future than to solve today's problems. After all, if you're wrong when the future you predicted comes to pass, who'll remember? But if you goof in the present everyone knows. Those who manage themselves daily and function in a solution-oriented environment will accomplish far more to help change the world than soothsayers who tell us why things will get worse. Give me the futurist who looks into the past for good news...finds and reports it. S/he gets my undivided attention. We need good news on a regular basis to counteract the brainwashing (stuffing?) we get from external sources. You can develop more inside strength by exposing yourself to those things which will match your personal philosophy, and internalizing them.

# Ninety Seven

# 48 Hours

No, this isn't about the TV show "48 hours". Rather, this answers the question of "When is a three-day weekend not a three-day weekend?" Obviously, when it is only 48 hours long. This is not a complaint, just an innocent observation. You see, we began our 3-day weekend at Friday 1PM when we left for the Poconos, and we returned at 1PM on Sunday...some 390 miles later. We supped at the inn we stayed at on Friday and Saturday nights. We breakfasted on Saturday and Sunday mornings at the same place, a gourmet paradise. The inn is called the Overlook Inn...and it's just one hundred years old. But its cuisine is as young and fresh as the apple cider they served with cookies and tea at 4 PM.

Since we spent part of Friday, all Saturday and part of Sunday at the inn, this is known as a 3-day weekender. So be it! We enjoyed the ride almost as much as the food. The leaves in Pennsylvania are just beginning to turn, so that we were met with a plethora of brilliant colors. The trees are gigantic, and at times we felt as though we were driving through tunnels of greens and golds and browns. It was truly awesome.

This short weekend brought to my mind an event which I witnessed many years ago, while still living in Brooklyn., . It was a Sunday morning and my friends and I were getting ready to go to Coney Island for the day. We passed many cars on several roads on our way to the subway (minus graffiti and crime in those days) and we watched in silent amazement as the car occupants ranted and raved at other cars for not moving fast enough. There was cursing as well, and the thought then occurred to me that *"pleasure should be acquired pleasantly!"* I was 17 at the time, but the lesson never strayed too far from my thinking. It doesn't make sense to plan a happy *event* and develop high blood pressure while agonizing over the details. Better to stay home. At least no one else gets hurt this way.

I have since then tried to plan all trips pleasantly. Both for business or vacations. Since I believe *attitude* is most important before undertaking anything new, I put mine in high gear while preparing for the forthcoming event. This positive attitude sometimes propels me past any negative vibes lurking in the background. Ignore the negative and many times it will just go away, like a temporary nightmare. A healthy self-esteem demands a cheery disposition, which in turn leads to happy times.

I shall long remember the beauty of these past 48 hours. In my lectures and seminars I always say "the past is over" and it is; but happy memories need not be. Sometimes they serve as a soothing balm during hectic days.

# Ninety Eight

# United Nation

The United States may certainly become a "kinder" and "gentler" nation sometime in its future. Right now there are only pockets which epitomize these qualities in the fabric we recognize as America. One such exception is found in the Poconos located in the hills of Pennsylvania. The differences between New York and PA became apparent as soon as we stopped for gas, when I was told to get the gas *first,* and pay *later!* My second surprise came when I asked for the key to the men's toilet. I did not need one. Finally, when I was thanked by the clerk and the owner both as I left...I realized that kinder and gentler people already exist in the U.S., and that all we need to do is clone them more often. Perhaps manners are catching...a sort of new and improved social disease which hopefully will infect more areas of this nation. At the inn where my wife, my son and I stayed the service was impeccable, something I usually expect in ethnic restaurants these days. I suspect we'll be visiting the Poconos again the near future. It feels terrific to be treated with respect and to be made to feel important.

The title above is United Nation...not nations because I believe in the old saying: "Physician, heal thyself". We must first re-establish our position as the leading moral nation in the world. Becoming kinder and gentler to those less fortunate begins the process. This means actively working with those most of us would like to sweep under our national rug. Prison inmates, the poor and the homeless are good places to start. The ill and the elderly also qualify for our attention. A kind word or action will go a long way with most of these to help establish a high level of communication. Once opened, mutual trust is sure to follow as the haves and have-nots develop new relationships with each other. A united nation can use the concept of synergy, wherein the combined strength of all our people is far stronger than strength used by millions on an *individual basis.* It's what made us Number 1 in the past.

Going back to the simple philosophy that all "persons" are created equal and must be treated thus will get the national ball rolling toward the U.S. goal-lines once again. Teaching children and teaching teachers and teaching religious leaders and teaching politicians...in other words teaching *everyone* who can affect our future as a country. That should be our short-range goal. Also, I suggest we erase state boundaries and learn to think of them as patches necessary to complete a very colorful, national quilt.

Let us remember that only change is constant, and that a rut is a coffin with the ends kicked out.

# Ninety Nine

# Artificial Intelligence

Artificial intelligence is an idea whose time has *gone!* Contrary to popular belief we have been using "artificial" intelligence for many centuries. Which is why the world is in such a turmoil. What we call A.I. is sometimes convoluted thinking. Examples abound daily. A famous Yankee baseball manager once said: "If people don't wanna come to the Stadium...how you gonna stop 'em?" Gives me a headache just trying to unknot this one. Also in England...a bus company. When the drivers went by long queues of waiting passengers at bus stops while their buses were half-empty here's their "intelligent" excuse: "We can't stop for passengers because it would interfere with our route schedules!" Need I say more?

Finally take the case of 3,000 people who developed mass blindness simultaneously. This happened in 1953 at Carswell Air Force Base (Ft. Worth, Texas) where I was stationed as a recreational specialist. I had worked on the opening of a new Airmen's Service Club for several months and tonight the ribbon would be cut by the base commander...followed by a beauty pageant which I had orchestrated to crown Miss Carswell. The sun had just set and the lights were turned on outside the new Service Club. Outside were over 3,000 Air Force personnel, their spouses and friends. The Service Club director had just finished introducing the base commander when it happened. Right by the microphone, in the main spotlight a couple of stray dogs decided to give the base a free show...and they did! And no one saw this...as the base commander bravely made his speech not two feet away! Was this mass hysteria..or were they using artificial intelligence, which negated their sense of sight? I never had the occasion to question them but I believe the dogs had as good a night as anyone there.

I think artificial intelligence is also used by what we call "common sense". I choose to live my life using uncommon sense...unpolluted by mass thinking and fueled from the innate, or spirit residing within me. I believe this is called "inspiration".

The proper use of mental energy is true intelligence in action. My dictionary defines intelligence as "the skilled use of reason." And as the great philosopher Sophocles (C.495-406 BC) wrote: "Reason is God's crowning gift to man!"

# One Hundred

# Space

I value space perhaps more than most of us do. I can remember feeling crowded most of my childhood years. It began in Brussels, Belgium where I was born. My parents, brother and I lived in a 2-room apartment. *I mean 2 rooms.* Bedroom and kitchen. The bathroom was in the hallway on a higher floor. The bedroom had two beds filling most of the floor space. One bed for my parents and one for my brother and I. In winter my mother used to iron our bedsheet for warmth just before we jumped into bed. There was no other heat affordable to us.

I do not remember the farm where we spent one month after escaping from the Nazis when they invaded Belgium. It was located in the southern part of France, near the city of Toulouse. The village was called Villaries; I have been unable to find it on maps of France.

We ran once again ending up in Casablanca, French Morocco. We stayed there for 3 years until the American invasion. While we were refugees in Casablanca we lived (the four of us) in a tiny room at Rue de Tunisie (#4B). Before this the French authorities placed us with 140 other displaced persons in *stables.* We slept in the horses' *stalls..*

We finally came to America in April 1943...with $25 given to us by a refugee relief organization. Once again an apartment with only 2 rooms plus a half-kitchen. My brother and I shared the living room with a foldout bed at night. The address was 440 Houston Street, in lower (poor) Manhattan.

After this we moved into a 3-room apartment in Williamsburg, Brooklyn. Again the living room became a bedroom at night for my brother and me.

Soon after graduating from Eastern District High School I fractured my left femur (thigh-bone) in two while diving for a shoestring catch at the Kent Avenue park. This time I had to share my room (ward) with 17 other people, all strangers to me. This unhappy episode lasted over 4 months...where in I had no privacy at all during the healing process.

Next came my four years in the Air Force where I had to share my sleeping quarters with 3 other airmen. Once again I was a "no-space" cadet. After my stint as a recreational specialist in Ft. Worth, Texas and Limestone (Maine) I was discharged from the service and began a search for space. I found the 92nd Street "Y" had rooms for singles...who came to study in the U.S. from all over the world. I put in for a room...and had to wait 10 months before I could call it home. Until then I did remain at home, with the famous foldaway bed waiting for me.

Now, *for the first time in my life*...at age 25 I owned my own room (roomette?). The bathroom was way down the hall and I did have to share it with over 50 other single tenants, but I had my own room! *Privacy at last.*

With over 100 girls occupying the two floors above mine...I finally slept alone!

My next step was to share my first apartment with another man from the "Y" on East 91st Street. The house was built in 1888 and I'm sure that I slept in the first bed installed there. My roommate was a singer/composer. This meant a steady procession into our apartment of men and women connected with the music publishing industry. Which is how I met my first wife.

She and I and her young son moved across Central Park to a new development...Park West Village. Finally the beginning of the American dream. A 19th floor apartment overlooking Central Park and a Lincoln in the parking lot. This as a result of my career with Encyclopaedia Britannica.

Many years later I sit in front of my word processor typing these nostalgic, albeit not always happy times. I have appropriated 1 1/2 rooms for my study/office/library in my new home and the view from my windows is spectacular. I can see the LILCO (Long Island Lighting Co.) chimneys 10 miles north of my home, as well as the Stony Brook Hospital northwest of here, 8 miles away.

I have space, and I can breathe fresh air by keeping my windows open.
*A very old goal finally coming to fruition.*

*To me every hour of the light and dark is a miracle,*
*every cubic inch of space a miracle.*

Walt Whitman

# One Hundred One

# Memories

For most of us memories should be relegated to the past, from whence they came.  Since a high majority of memories are mental repeats of negative experiences and conditioning they belong in a dust heap of the past. Having had a less than desirable childhood in 4 different countries I can attest to the fact that *most memories hurt like hell!*

For example Brussels, Belgium where I was born.  I remember the nuns in schools (which were all Catholic) hitting my left hand, forcing me to become right-handed...a crime against Nature.  I also recall a lay teacher in Brussels who punished the students by inserting our index finger in a bird cage.  We had to keep it there until the big blackbird pecked at it and drew blood.  Another nice way to begin my education.

In Casablanca, Morocco the Arab teacher used a cat-o-nine tails to keep us in order.  Finally in a parochial school in Brooklyn the rabbi used a heavy ruler across our knuckles when we did not learn our lesson at *his desired speed and level of accuracy*.  And I thought learning was supposed to be fun!

Getting back to memories the preeminent psychologist Dr. Maxwell Maltz said we live 60% of our awake time thinking in the past.  The past is over...yet we cling to it as though for life!  Sounds mighty dangerous doesn't it?  Yet this is what we do when living in the past.  The good-feelings memories help to shore up our sagging self-esteem but the bad ones drag us down...and keep us operating at a very low level of achievement.

If it's true that we become as we think about all day long we had better change our act, and think of Positive Solutions to life rather than how we failed in the past at something.  *We reinforce the negatives each time we give them a new life by remembering them.*  Use them once as a fulcrum to propel you into a better future, than let go of them!  Their power is defused by using bad memories as something you don't want to happen again.

Your good past empowers you to repeat that happening for...as Marcus Valerius Martialis (A.D.40-104) said:  "...he lives two lives who relives his past with pleasure!"

May you then live many lives by recalling only your pleasurable past.

# *One Hundred Two.*

# Polyticks

No, this is not a misspelling...instead, it's a metaphor I carefully chose to illustrate today's politics. Polyticks, or *many ticks* remind me of politicians as a genre. First, both of them try to latch on to their "victims" (voters?) with a near-death grip. Then both proceed to bleed their "hosts" until satiated...Politicians take a little longer, i.e., 2, 4 or 6 years.

A wit once remarked that if we were to take all politicians and line them up on the ground, touching head to toe for miles on end, it would be a wonderful thing! What a great idea to get them out of the way.

Voting, in this writer's humble opinion has become for the most part a question of choosing the lesser evil. I have become very disillusioned with what now passes for the *"will of the people"*. In the White House, now the heavily "Tainted House" the political lies pile up faster than the national deficit. And the American public continues to lead with its collective chin. Reminds me of the guy walking around with a *kick me* sign on his back. The problem is: *he put the sign on himself.*

I have a simple solution..which is why it will never be implemented. Hold politicians responsible for their promises. If I yell fire in a crowded theater I am accountable. I lied, and must pay the price. Well, let's make politicians honest for a change.

I know the old argument. Many will disappear under the woodwork. Which is where they probably belong. The honest ones will stay, and continue to do good work by truly servicing the public which is trusting them with their welfare.

Either make them accountable for their words and deeds, or let's go back to a more basic way of choosing them. Throwing darts while blindfolded...at a board with all the candidates' names on it. Chances are, we won't be "off the mark" by much.

I just want to be able to vote and sleep nights, knowing the job is being done according to promises made *before I dropped the lever in the booth.* My hopes are equal to those of John Adams in his letter to Abigail on November 2, 1800: "I pray Heaven to bestow the best of blessings on this house...May none but honest and wise (wo)men ever rule under this roof". I am not yet uncrossing my fingers.

*One Hundred Two.*

# Schools

According to a recent survey at the University of Miami 100 students were asked where London was. 42 out of the 100 did not know. The same 100 were shown a map of the United States; 8 of them could not find Miami. *(They were in Miami at the time).* In 1990 37% of New Jersey freshmen failed a verbal-skills test; 58% flunked an algebra test. In the past six years over half the college students at 4-year institutions have dropped out. Community colleges fare even worse.

The attitudes of both teachers and pupils in general run parallel to each other, i.e., lower levels of personal motivation. One problem is, we concentrate too much on the Fs rather than the As...and students react accordingly. By Fs I refer to *facts, figures & formulas*, rather than As for *attitude, appreciation, acceptance, approval & admiration.* The National PTA recently pointed out that for each Positive stroke given by a teacher to a pupil, an average of 18 Negative strokes will be inflicted on that same pupil from the same tutorial source. In '87, the same National PTA ranked self-esteem as the #1 problem with students, and recommended the schools work on this more diligently. Four years later the problem is worse. Two main reasons are: first, teachers are not improving their own self-esteem. (A perfect case for physicians heal thyself) Second, parents have turned over this all-important job to the school system, thereby walking away from it altogether. With mediocrity now becoming the norm all students suffer, including the good ones. In January 1990 the state of California published "Toward A State of Esteem". Under *"Key Findings"* the report (144 pages) states: The lack of self-esteem is central to most personal and social ills plaguing our state and nation as we approach the end of the twentieth century...The family is the incubator of self-esteem and the most crucial social unit in a child's life and development...Since children spend so much of their time in school, the environment of the school also plays a major role in the development of self-esteem.

Under "Key Recommendations" we find:...educate *all* Californians regarding the primary role of parents in the healthy development of healthy self-esteem...Every school district in California should adopt the promotion of self-esteem...integrated into its total curriculum...Course work in self-esteem should be required for credentials and as a part of ongoing in-service training for all educators.

There you have it!...Spelled out in black and white. *Both parents and teachers* must share the awesome responsibility if we are once more to emerge as a model nation. Just as it takes both wheels of a bicycle going in the same direction, at the same time, so should the parents and schools work in tandem for optimum results. Parents can begin by eliminating the 8 Negatives they give for each Positive stroke. This research also comes from the National PTA.

Learning, to be effective should be pleasurable, *even fun.* For both the teacher and the pupil. Tedium kills creativity, as do criticism and condemnation. Enthusiasm, tedium's deadly enemy must be everpresent in the classroom.

When TV first came out it was hailed as the greatest tool for mass education. The prediction proved perfect, as most programs teach us that human value is nil, that only the big "I" matters, and the trick is to get as much as you can for as little effort as possible.

Unfortunately, young minds are like the proverbial parachute. You only get one change to "open it" the right way!

Edmund Burke (1729-1797) finalizes this vignette with a powerful adage: "Example is the school of mankind, and they will learn at no other".

# *One Hundred Four*

# Writing

Why do I love to write? I believe writing can be the most powerful, personal, permanent way to lasting, effective communication.

Writing is powerful when its main purpose is to incite, excite, exhilarate, aggravate or frustrate; in other words...to touch us where we "live", negatively or positively.

Writing becomes personal when used as a one-on-one communicative tool, wherein the most intimate thoughts can be shared without being in front of the reader. Through someone's writing I can walk into the author's mind (or authoress) and explore it at will, to my heart's delight. I feel that writing truly reaches its peak when used to enhance the readers' self-esteem and personal image. Also, when used as a means to entertain through a classical tale, or immortal poetry.

The beauty of writing is its timeless permanence, so that all mankind can benefit from the thoughts of current as well as previous great thinkers and philosophers.

Good writing unites writer and reader with an artistic cord, invisible yet stronger than any steel cable. It touches generic human emotions and responses shared by all of us, male and female, young and old alike. It transcends time and space, as well as physical barriers.

Writing can also be used to heal, or hurt. Its power lies in the ability of certain words to make us feel good or bad about ourselves or situations we are involved in. Imaginative blending of verbs, adverbs, adjectives and metaphors can bring the author into our presence, as the impact of his well-chosen words hits us. For example, you can change the trite, well-worn and over-used phrase *"I love you"* into a power-packed, emotionally loaded sentence full of meaning by using a little ingenuity. It can easily become *"I truly love you very deeply!* " thereby touching the reader at the very core of his/her being.

I must be very careful to mix thinking and feeling in my work, or Shakespeare will have been prophetic when he wrote in Hamlet:

"My words fly up, my thoughts remain below:

Words without thoughts never to heaven go".

# One Hundred Five

# The Brain

The best description I have run across for the brain is: "A universal receiving station attached to a limitless bio-computer." Wow! Now that is a description worth remembering. If the Stanford University study is correct, and the average person uses no more than 2% of his/her potential...what are we dong with the rest? *Think* (no pun intended) *about that for a moment.*

One good analogy which comes to mind is that of your car, and the way you drive it. Suppose it had 100 horsepower under the hood, of which you used only 2. If your car was able to go at speeds of 100 MPH, you would be doing 2 MPH as long as you owned that car. A 1 HP increase in speed would in reality be a 50% increase in the result...3 MPH. The same is true of us. By just using 1/100th more of our capabilities we would increase the end result by 50%, and thus use 3% of our human potential.

The trick to being able to do this is to remove the mental governor we've saddled our minds with. Just as the car could not move beyond its 2 MPH with a governor attached to its gas pedal, neither can we advance to greater accomplishments without its removal. Our governor is the *sum total of all the negatives* we have piled into our subconscious. Since we cannot remove the negatives, we must instead use a force against them...i.e. positive, health-enhancing ideas and concepts. These attitudinal booster shots will push the mental governor away, and allow us the full freedom needed for personal growth. Fortunate are those few of us (3-5%) who are not victims of negative pre-conditioning. They become the doers...not the talkers of success and happy living. Age, size, color, religion do not interfere with their high self-esteem, which enables them to be winners at anything they attempt. Two great examples come to mind, in the sports field. The first is Nolan Ryan, the 44 year old pitcher who recently pitched his seventh no-hitter. The second example comes from the animal kingdom, for they also use brains. John Henry is not the beautiful thoroughbred we are accustomed to seeing at the race track. He is short, deepchested, and 14 years old. Yet he keeps winning horseraces against the young, slim 2 and 3 year olds. *His mind has not accepted his physical limitations.* Can you do the same as a humble horse?

# One Hundred Six

# Media

It took an act of the Chief Justice of the Supreme Court to get me off the "Good Morning America" show. In June 1986, Warren E. Berger cancelled my appearance on the show by resigning his post, on which he had served with honor since 1969. "GMA" felt this development was more important on a national level than my interview would be on its program. The odds of his resigning on my day for national recognition were 6,200 to 1 (the # of days he served). I had to be content with the Regis Philbin Show, ABC-News and CBS-News, as well as a full page in the NY Post, a questionable honor at best. What, you may wonder, had I done to deserve this momentary fame? It's really very simple. I became the *first male president of a woman's business club in the history of NY State.* After a 2-hour interview Newsday, in its infinite wisdom decided it was not newsworthy. They did not care for my explanation on why I had chosen to run and win the presidency. I said: "I was discriminated against because of my religion in Belgium and had to run to save my life. Now I have a chance to fight against sex discrimination, and I'm anxious to win!"

However, what did happen is the reason for this little tale. Both ABC and CBS featured me on their 6 o'clock News programs, but only after both had exhausted their *bad news first!* I counted ten negative news items on one channel and eleven on the other; then came the only "positive" of the hour. This time, luck was on my side. Had there occurred one more bad news item, I'm sure my story would have been "bumped" and sent into obscurity once more. My point is; bad news is "news"...good news is used as "fillers" by the media.

I once counted the good/news vs. bad/news occurring in two major newspapers with very high circulations. Bad news won by a margin of 9.5 to 1. As a nation we are heading precipitously into an abyss of negativity which will soon begin to feed on itself, and eventually consume itself. We are building our own little atomic bombs, filled with bad news instead of atoms. Headlines are used instead of detonators, but the final effect is the same. Some decent little part of us is destroyed each time we add to our personal storage tank, as we fill it daily with *negative affirmations.* We need to begin systematic mental inputs of positive ideas and ideals before we become totally immersed in stinkin' thinkin', as Zig Ziglar calls it.

I'm still old-fashioned enough to believe we are made in God's image, spiritually. It behooves us to behave in ways which will not discredit this noble inheritance. Following is a letter I wrote to Newsday, for their "500 Words or Less" column:

# One Hundred Seven

# I Cry For America

On May 14, exactly 50 years ago my parents, brother and I ran from the Nazis. We were living in Brussels, Belgium where I was born. Passover had just ended the week before and once again Jews were running, carrying only the "matzohs" they could carry with them. The new Diaspora, circa 1940. Our goal was the USA, where many relatives already lived. Instead, we ended up as refugees in Casablanca, Morocco.

On April 9, 1943 we became the first WW2 displaced persons to reach America. At that time it was the role model for the world. Pride, Purpose and Patriotism poured out of this nation of immigrants, inspiring others to emulate it.

A very short half-century later the 3 Ps have become Perks, Prescriptions and Procrastination. We now lead the world in crime, attempted suicides, abortions, runaway teenagers, drug and drinking problems, divorces and unethical business practices. We have lost both our economic and educational edges. Readin', Ritin' and 'Rithmetic have become Ritual, Rut 'n Routine. Big Business and Bigger Government have cut deeply into our once naive trust, and our national motto could now read: "What's in it for Me?"

In just 50 years we have lost the "moral war", as well as our status as #1 Nation.

I cried in 1943 when I first saw the statue of Liberty, but those were tears of joy!

In the past 24 months I have listened to over 7,800 people in more than 35 states who attended seminars I conducted on *customer satisfaction*. What they said chagrined me, for everywhere I went the same theme occurred. People are no longer treating or being treated as human beings. Feelings are left out of most interpersonal communications; instead, *rudeness and brusqueness abound* in both the business world, as well as in the private areas of our lives. When I asked the attendees what they wanted out of life (including their jobs) their most pressing needs were: respect, appreciation, praise, being listened to, acceptance, feeling important, being loved, and being understood. *Their need for money ranked below all the above.*

It appears as though much of the initial parental nurturing is missing from their lives, due to the growing need for 2-income families. Also, the media is waging a full-scale war with consumers, making them feel inferior if they do not purchase the "in" items in order to bolster their sagging self-esteems. The National PTA tells us that between parents and teachers children average 13 negative strokes for each positive reinforcement to their self-image. Culturally our original "melting pot" of the world concept has been replaced by new ghettos separating the whites, blacks, orientals and others.  As a result, racial and ethnic discrimination continue to increase.

*I cry again today for America*, because my dream is shattered and America no longer follows its Manifest Destiny.  It has lost the sense of Purpose which once made it the greatest nation in the history of mankind.

I long once again for the days when we can exhibit true Pride in our workplace, as well as honest Patriotism in our nation.  Only then will we recapture our rightful place in the sun.

P.S. *This also was not published by Newsday, Long Island's only major newspaper.*  (Perhaps I should change my deodorant!)

It says in the Good Book, Acts 8:32...

*The truth shall make you free.*

# One Hundred Eight

# Reunion

A 40-year hiatus ended for me last month, when my old high school (Eastern District H.S.) held its 40th reunion for the classes of 1950-51. I had not been in touch with anyone of my graduation class, since I had gone into the Air Force in 1952 for a four-year stint. For some strange reason my mind stood still as I looked for my friends among those attending the festive occasion. I thought, irrationally I'm sure, that everyone would look the same as they did in 1951. Imagine my surprise when I spotted old friends...*looking old!* Some had white hair, some no hair. The ladies were now mature, and showed the facial lines of *grandmotherhood*. But the eyes...how they sparkled! Ran into my first girlfriend, and also my best girl friend. My closest buddy and his wife of 34 years. There was enough hugging and kissing done this night to last me until our 50th reunion, which is already being planned for. Coincidentally, my other recollection of a great reunion is when I celebrated my 40th birthday. This was the year I gave out more presents than I received from my guests. Were they ever surprised! It was my best birthday ever. Try it! My next "special" reunion took place in Scottsdale, Arizona in July 1984. The *National Speakers Association* was holding its annual convention there, and I was asked to give an invocation at lunchtime before 1,000 speakers. Since the World Olympics were being held in Los Angeles at that same time I decided to use their five-ring symbol as my outline.

Following is the exact invocation I delivered before my peers:

The World Olympics are now in progress...and I'd like to suggest that the U.S. Olympic Committee left out one important category...Speakers!...for we here are the finalists of our profession. Think for a moment of the 5-ring Olympic symbol. To speakers the rings can stand for:

1- our know-how
2- our energy
3- our time
4- our imagination, and finally
5- our ability to communicate!

Put them together as rings and you have Unity and Strength...which equals power! *The power concentrated in this room is truly unlimited.* As members of the NSA we can literally change the world. Here's how...The NSA now numbers over 2,500 members...if each one of us speaks an average of 100 times per year to groups of 100 or more, we in this room can touch 25 million lives per year...or all the adults in the U.S. in 5 years!

As professional speakers we have the power to move people to action!...By interweaving philosophical ideals into our lectures and seminars we can help re-instill the qualities which made this nation great...such as Honesty, Integrity, Love and the Work-Ethic!...I say, educate your clients, and *love 'em to life!* (not death)

The word invocation means to ask for help, usually of a Divine source. Since the Greeks had many gods I shall borrow the following quote from one of them:

*"Whatever kind of word thou speakest...the like shalt thou hear!"*

I began this vignette discussing the age of my friends. And how old some of them looked. As a lecturer/writer of Positive Living I find my physical/mental age nowhere near my chronological age. I actually looked forward to my 40th, my 50th and now my upcoming 60th birthdays, since they do not relate to my *attitudinal age,* with its child-like eagerness for life.

I like what Sir William Temple had to say about age in his ANCIENT AND MODERN LEARNING...written in 1690: "Books, like proverbs, receive their chief value from the stamp and esteem of ages through which they have passed". I think the same can be said of people!

# *One Hundred Nine*

# Campus Life

"He who enters a University walks on hallowed ground"...once said James B. Conant. This inspiring phrase was completely lost on me last week as I walked through Nassau Community College. I was there to deliver a lecture on motivation to a night class.

Although the campus is only a few years old it can already be classified as a pig-sty. It seems as though our current generation has such a low self-esteem it cannot conceive learning in a beautiful environment. Many of the students' clothes matched the "inferior decoration" of the buildings; the same students whom we have chosen as our investment for the future.

Since parents give us our original "food for thought" I think it's important to know what kind of a mental diet we're being fed these days. One major study, undertaken by the White House Conference on Children had over 4,000 delegates attending from all over the United States. The final report was *a unanimous indictment of our nation for its vast neglect of children.* It shattered once and for all the myth that this is a child-oriented society. Too many parents use love (or withhold it) as a manipulative tool to control their offspring, to keep them on course. A course defined by the needs of the parents...not the children. With prices going out of sight and divorces topping the 50% mark, we find a new mood in those who are responsible for the raising of their young ones...*rage!* Since we're no longer a farm-dominated nation less children are needed, and there are fewer ways they can help pay for their expensive room and board.

The point is...if your non-verbal signals belie what you say to your sons and daughters, don't be surprised if they grow up and do the same to you now and to their own children later. As one prominent psychologist put it: *most talking is a lie.* Regardless of what a parent says the child will respond to the non-verbal messages, and the tone used. What this boils down to is really quite simple. Children are small human beings. They have the same needs, hungers and wants as do grownups...but on a smaller scale. Just as physical food helps them to grow into personhood, so does the mental diet we dish out to them daily.

Parents have unlimited opportunities to improve our nation's future by being *positive examples* to their children. Eliminating words like "stupid", "clumsy", "dope"...would be a good start. Throughout history we have dumped on them, as we passed our low self-esteem along with our genes from generation to generation. I strongly suggest a reawakening of the parental conscience, and a renewed dedication to children who someday will also become parents. The fate of America rests on the new leadership, which will come from the ranks of ex-children.

# One Hundred Ten

# Positive Action=Positive Living

I just had lunch with a lovely, attractive and very bright woman. The only problem is that she is very overweight, and this makes her life miserable. Know anybody like that? Sure...we all do. *She says she hates being fat.* She's been to WW, OA and many doctors in the past. The doctors always give her pills to take. Funny, but I don't remember ever becoming overweight by eating too many pills. (And I've been there a "bad" part of my life) Pills do not correct habits, and overeating is a self-destructive habit. New and stronger habits eliminate old habits. Not pills. Pills do guarantee future business for doctors, as they keep switching from one type to another, hoping to find the "magic potion". At great expense to us, both emotionally and financially. Also, why would anyone want to go and mingle at WW and OA with other "fatties" in order to lose weight? Not too many role models to look up to. Try instead going to a series of meetings with only skinny people and see how fast you'll drop the weight...since you won't want to "stick out" like a sore thumb in a group of peers.

Please remember that nobody became fat in groups, but on an individual basis only. Group sessions are great if you want to commiserate with peers, and dwell on the difficulties involved in weight loss. For example: If you only lost one pound the past week isn't it great to find someone who only lost 1/2 lb. You may feel better comparing yourself to others, but this will not help solve *your problem.*

Overeating resolves temporary stress situations for many of us, but creates new, permanent problems, which become more difficult to deal with. The same holds true of smoking, drinking, pill-taking, etc...wherein the habit acquired solved a minor problem and became a greater one. What then is the answer to the distress we cause ourselves by seeking these "short-term" remedies? The answer lies within the self, which originally created the habit, and then allowed it to grow beyond our control.

For example my lady friend told me she begins to eat impulsively the moment a crisis occurs in her life (a child becomes ill, or husband goes on a long business trip, etc.)...or anything that ruffles the smooth path of her life. I'm sure that she, like me, can boast of having lost herself several times in body weight through past diets. Since none of that weight was lost forever...each time it came back it reinforced the horrible fact that we can't lost weight...and so we gain...and lose...and gain...and lose...until our weight chart begins to look like the Swiss Alps with all its peaks and valleys.

How then do we break a habit which we do not have, but rather *has us?* The answer sounds simple, but the doing far more difficult. The reason to break the habit and become thinner *must be stronger* than the reason to keep it! My friend thought that she was overeating to get even with those who caused her stress. If her dad gets sick and it interferes with her personal life she becomes angry and worries. To get even with him for creating the anguish she "oinks out" knowing this in turn will make him angry and worried. Eventually dad gets well, but my friend retains the new weight. Who gained (pun?) by this exchange of psychological games? *Mentally her self-esteem gets even lower...and physically her weight even higher.*

What price revenge?

I truly believe that because she was brought up with a healthy set of ethics (Honor thy father, etc...) she feels guilty for being selfish *(her exact word)*. A perfect reason for the self-destruct act of pigging out. Seems to be a "Catch 22" situation, doesn't it? One way to resolve this dilemma and get off the mental treadmill (going nowhere fast) and recognize the selfish feeling as a throwback to our childhood, when it was needed for survival. As a grownup she can understand her father's illness as natural...and not something he uses to punish her in any way. With understanding comes patience, and through patience she then develops compassion for him. She can now handle the situation as an adult without resorting to infantile urges (i.e. overeat...to show him).

When you no longer try to punish yourself for these feelings Self-Esteem dictates an increased self-respect for your body...and you'll become thinner, more attractive. You now learn to like yourself more and feel worthy of your new, improved body.

Hives, ulcers, shingles, nervous tension,high blood pressure et al are the heavy price we pay for unresolved traumas which include anger, hatred, fear, envy and thoughts of revenge. In order to live with "peace of mind" in this world these feelings cannot usually be outer-directed toward others. Therefore we channel them inwardly and pay the price for not wanting to grow up. My friend also told me that she was on the way to meet some of the "girls" later that day. These people who insist on being treated by others as adults persist on labeling themselves "girls" (ergo they age from 35 to 85).

If I might take poetic license for a moment and paraphrase William Shakespeare: "To be grownup, or not be be...that is the question. Whether 'tis nobler to remain a child and suffer many indignities because our bodies outdistanced our minds...etc."

In order to change one personal habit for a new and better one you must first visualize *the person you want to become.* Vividly, and with great detail. Then, for 30 days record each time you engage in your bad habit the feelings which led you to the despised act. You'll soon uncover a common bond which unites your erratic behavior. When you do, ask yourself if your response is not only immature, but outdated as well now that you are a grownup.

Next...when your habit raises its ugly head wait 15 minutes before you indulge in it. During this time, visualize the person you want to be, and repeat to yourself the new reason for getting off the past. By the time the 15 min. are over you'll find very often that your time bomb (habit) has been diffused, with no emotional explosion.

It's also very important to use short-range goals when kicking a negative habit out of your life. Don't try to lose 10 lbs. in one week. Several years ago I became 38 lbs. thinner in 38 weeks...one pound per week, with no real diet or regimen. Just cut 5-10% of my calorie intake and continued to eat the same foods as before. No struggle or nervousness. Of course at the time I also *released and forgave a host of people who had hurt me in the past!!!* Imagine 38 lbs. of anger and hatred being carried around for so many years. Before this I had tried every diet in the book and some still unpublished. On my annual calendars Sunday was followed by Dietday, etc...This time I decided to give myself a fair chance at winning the battle of the "bulge" by only eliminating one pound per week. This gave me constant positive reinforcement needed for Success...and it worked! The combination of forgiveness plus low goals did the job permanently. I don't have to tell you what this did for my self-image.

Once again: make sure the reason to become thinner is stronger than the reason to keep the extra avoirdupois. And what better reason can you possibly have than to feel you deserve a healthy body because you got rid of the mental poisons!

I recommend using this technique when angry or frustrated because somebody DARED to have a different opinion than yours, or had the NERVE to defy your wishes. I use these two words in capitals on purpose (with a little sarcasm) since people usually want to do their own thing! And this may not coincide with yours. They are not picking on you...just looking for their own space. Allow people this freedom and they will be glad to give you your space as well. Let's think about this for a moment. If there were no other opinions in the world but yours, there would only be 1 way to do things. 1 style of furniture; 1 color for curtains; 1 topic of conversation (you); 1 style of cooking (this past month I've been to Chinese, Greek, French, Italian, Thai, Spanish, Deli and Japanese restaurants). There would only be 1 model car, 1 newspaper, 1 school, 1 TV channel, etc...*How boring life would then become.* There would be mass unemployment, since only 1 style of everything would be manufactured. Having one political party (dictatorial?) doesn't thrill me either. How about one race, one religion or one color. Which would you choose? Which would you eliminate? This "melting pot" named the U.S. has given the world a diversity of talent, music, art, goods and services unparalleled in history. Let's keep and make good use of the "differences" among us, because *variety is the spice of life!*

Positive Living means living comfortably in our own space, while allowing others to live in theirs...albeit unlike ours. After all, to them ours is the different one. Different does not mean worse, or better...just different! *Vive la difference!*

# One Hundred Eleven

# The Generation .....Chasm

How would you like to know what our next generation thinks in certain major areas?  After all our future leaders will come from these ranks.  I recently finished reading a survey taken for TEEN MAGAZINE.  The results were to say the least, unsettling.  The teenage boys rated their female counterparts in the following manner:  the top 3 spots went for the girl who was

a- interested in *him*

b- loyal to *him*

c- considerate and thoughtful of *him*

Talk about adolescent insecurities!  Spots #9 and #10 were checked for Assertiveness and Intelligence, in that order.  After all we can't have the girls smarter than their dates.  Bodies are in and minds are out.  If you are still a doubter watch the TV ads.  We don't sell much for the brain; therefore we stress the bodily needs of our young, new consumers.  The facial feature the guys found most appealing is the eyes (53%).  Small wonder, since the eyes can telegraph intelligence, or the lack thereof!  The modern, liberated girl rated 16th in the survey.

The boys were then asked what they thought the girls looked for in them.  Here's what we found.  Good looks and muscular builds came in first and second.  *Intelligence did not even make it to the top 10.*  With this highly distorted sense of values being programmed into this new generation the following facts are not too surprising.  According to a report in the early 80's in U.S. News and World Report we have well over 10 million juveniles and young adults involved with the criminal justice system...and over 14 million have varying degrees of emotional problems, are severely disturbed or are retarded.  And this in the most scientifically enlightened nation in the world...dedicated to the "pursuit of happiness!"

A Time Magazine poll showed that better than 3 out of 4 people want the morning prayers restored in the school system.  Perhaps the prayers should be *for* the schools, where teacher burnout is at an all time high.  It is not their job to teach ethics and morality, but they should be able to *reinforce* these time-tested values.  As should the keepers of our moral treasures, i.e. the ministers, priests and rabbis.

But the bottom line still underscores the parental need to teach by example what's right, wrong, important or not.  When we came to America in 1943 my parents enrolled in night school immediately in order to learn the language of their new home.  Now, parents should sign up for classes in ethics, self-esteem, child psychology, etc...in order to renew their skills in dealing with their troubled children.

# One Hundred Twelve

# The Gap

My favorite quote of all is the one by Wolfgang Von Goethe (1749-1832). It reads as follows: "If we take people as they are we make them worse. If we treat them as if they were what they ought to be, we help them to become what they are capable of being!" If we could just remember this one and apply it daily it would be the end of arguments, disagreements and wars. Perhaps this is why we believe there will always be war. When high school students, undergraduates and adults were surveyed on the question of war...3 out of 5 agreed with the statement: "Human nature being what it is, there will always be war."

In the past many researchers concluded that violence is inherent in human nature. And yet the latest research done by some of the world's leading ethologists, psychologists and neurophysiologists showed clearly the opposite. Some of their findings:

a-*It is scientifically incorrect to say that humans have a "violent" brain.*

b-It is scientifically incorrect to say that war or any other violent behavior is genetically programmed into our human nature.

c-It is scientifically incorrect to say that war is caused by instinct or any other single motivation.

Thus the Seville Statement (Spain) concludes that biology does not condemn humanity to war, or biological pessimism through genetic heredity. Men, the inventors of war can become the inventors of peace. Let's put the theory of natural aggressiveness in man to rest once and for all, thus closing the gap between theory and reality.

Which brings us to another dilemma. What excuse do men have now for continuing the insane wars that are always breaking out somewhere on our planet? If we are truly the wards of this earth by what logical thinking can we solve social and economic problems by waging war on other nations? It seems we need to do some re-thinking about the true causes and effects of war.

My family and I ran from the Germans as they were bombing a tiny nation into submission. Belgium had done nothing to invite mass destruction, but became a pawn in the game of European politics. As a result we lost all we had, for we ran from Brussels carrying only what we could on our backs and in our hands. I was 7 years old, hardly able to understand why we had to run from a nation which threatened extermination for those of my religion who remained behind and were caught. *Talk about pure insanity!*

This experience gave me an aversion to any war, and continues to gnaw at my gut each time I read of another conflict beginning on one continent or another.

The Seville report, written in the late 80s should be read and studied by all the members of the United Nations. Once we fully understand that war is outdated we can concentrate on the human potential, which remains for the most part undisturbed in our unconscious mind. The greatest goal for the UN can be the bridging of the gap between *what humans are today and what they can become tomorrow.* Only then will "loving they neighbor" really mean something. Because of our new and immediate communications abilities, our current "neighbor" can be anyone who resides on this planet. How can we help at the local level? That's easy...begin by loving yourself, thus paving the way for loving others.

A final word on war comes from the eminent physicist Max Born who died at age 88. He wrote in June 1957 in the Bulletin of Atomic Scientists the following warning:

"The human race has today the means for annihilating itself - either in a fit of complete lunacy, i.e. in a big war, by a brief fit of destruction, or by careless handling of atomic technology, through a slow process of poisoning and of deterioration in its genetic structure".

# *One Hundred Thirteen*

# Do-Did-Get-Got

The law of the universe is really very simple. It states that "if you proceed to do what you did in the past, you'll continue to get what you got". *No exceptions.* This means that if you like where you are in life's journey, don't change anything except your daily underwear. If on the other hand you're looking ahead to a better future than the past has been...mental modifications will have to be made, consistent with where you now want to go against where you've been.

I just finished doing two one-day seminars with the customer service reps of a large chain of appliance and electronics stores located on Long Island. The women involved were of all ages and different levels of experience. And yet, a common bond appeared as we discussed who the typical irate client calling them was. It seems as though the CSRs (Customer Service Reps) finally recognized themselves as also being the tough, angry customer in another frame of time and place. Therefore by learning more about who they (CSRs) were, they began to understand the client. With understanding came *empathy*, a quality needed for successful problem-solving by phone.

These women quickly grasped the concept that *they*...and not the customer had to change during the confrontation. This way they became more able to control the conversation and guide the complainant into a reasonable solution, while dissipating their initial anger. The women finally understood that suffering on this high-stress job *is an option* they can choose not to exercise and become more productive instead. The bottom line is that for all intent and purposes, everyone we communicate with is for the moment our customer...who will either "buy" or reject the intent of our communication with them.

Some of the women were astute enough to suggest that what we did for a full-day was just the *tip of the iceberg* when learning to deal with people. I could only agree and hope the company will continue with motivational and skills-enhancement programs, since they work like vitamins do...only if you take them on a regular basis.

When we shared the latest ideas on breaking down the walls which inhibit solid interpersonal dialogues the women beamed. The reason soon became clear: They were anxious to try the techniques on their children, spouses, lovers, in-laws and friends. They felt they had a new tool which could be applied successfully to an old problem. Although they had done much of the uncovery work with me, they applauded at the end of the day. You see, we were talking about their favorite subject...*them*...and they were eager participants. They will now use the knowledge that angry customers are really CSRs *turned inside out*, therefore like them.

# One Hundred Fourteen

# The Symphony of Life

Music is to the mind, brain or soul as food is to the body. The music you listen to can help determine the degree of happiness you will reach in your life. Some music parallels the role vitamins play in our health. My favorite music is the classical kind written by composers whose lives were touched with genius. Therein lies the analogy. You are the conductor of *the symphony of life.* Your orchestra is composed of 4 major sections...strings, brass, percussion and woodwinds.

If you attach each musical section to a part of your life, you may end up with the following metaphor: since the strings deliver the lightest and most beautiful sounds they represent your *spiritual side.* The brass can represent your *physical life.* Percussion covers your *mental development* and finally, woodwinds allegorize *your career.* As the symphonic conductor you have the opportunity to make each performance unforgettable. This is done by synchronizing the four sections, each playing its part in perfect rhythm and in tune with the others. The result is truly satisfying every time.

The same concept holds true for your life. A careful blend of the four important areas governing your daily activities will result in a *stress-free environment.* We were all given the same music sheet at birth. It's what we do with the score that counts in the long run. Some of us take it out of its envelope once in a great while, and wonder why life hands us the dirty end of the stick. Others never even see it once, and die with the music still in them. Luckily some of us remember about it in time to change our lives.

This means a reappraisal of our values, which include our work ethic, honesty and integrity. Also, it involves the qualities of empathy, patience and compassion for others...as well as the *ability to forgive.* I think it's high time we accepted the fact that there is no white knight in sight to rescue us from a boring, unproductive life. Actually, the knight turned into a modern couch potato suffering from hemorrhoids, and not very reliable.

Putting your act together means thinking about spiritual, mental, physical and career goals as *one*, differing only in their intensity. It includes writing down what you want to accomplish in all these areas, with dates and necessary life-changes. Once this is on paper, both left and right brains know what your plans are, and can proceed *as one* to deliver.

In his "Seed for Thought" Charles Kettering (1876-1958) wrote: "We should all be concerned about the future because we will have to spend the rest of our lives there". Concerned, yes...worried, no. Not if you know where you're going. Having concrete plans in the major areas of life gives one self-confidence, a much needed bromide in these difficult times. Play your symphony as if your life depends on it because *it does!*

# One Hundred Fifteen

# What I Have Learned

As I pass page 600 in my original manuscript on life I noticed I finally developed a philosophy I can live by. I don't know what yours is, but I feel it is time to share some major premises I use to keep my personal ship afloat while sailing through the muddied waters of life. You've heard of Buddha's Noble Eight-Fold Path. Well, I have my own eight-pack which I carry around in my bicameral mind.

1- We create every so-called "disease" in our body. Enough research has shown that releasing resentment will dissolve even the dreaded *cancer*. Usually, our body mirrors the patterns of negative thoughts and translates them into sickness which can even end in death.

2- *Condemnation, criticism and guilt* do the most damage to our health. Both criticism and condemnation start within us and do their destructive work on the outside before coming back with a vengeance inside the body of the original sender. Guilt is the direct result of doing something we know to be wrong and hurtful in some way to someone else, and for which we must pay a price.

3- Remember that thoughts can be controlled...and changed. We don't have the power to keep certain thoughts from creeping into our consciousness, but we can *immediately* change them, thus guaranteeing a healthy mind-set at all times.

4- Everyone suffers to some degree from guilt and self-hatred. The trick here is to eliminate these self-consuming thoughts by finding other people to help in some way, turning self-hatred into self-praise.

5- We are fully responsible for all the experiences in our lives. The universe works on a cause and effect principle. Break the natural laws and you pay the price. Some call this the law of karma.

6- The only power you wield is in the present moment. Today is all there is, so nurture it carefully. There is no yesterday, since you can't go into the past. Also, there is no tomorrow...since tomorrow becomes today when you finally reach it.

7- When we finally love ourselves, everything works in life! When a person learns to love himself, s/he can no longer be angry or hurtful toward another human being. As a result, life takes on a new dimension, bigger and better than ever before.

8- The above ideas only work when you work them! "Actions speak louder than words". Not a mere platitude, but a short sentence full of power and meaning. *Do the act* and you'll become the person. Don't mistake activity for achievement. Looking busy while repeating old acts are a complete waste of time and motion. Better to advance cautiously but steadfastly in one direction...changing one bad habit at a time. This will give you the self-acceptance necessary for further encouragement.

Ovid (43 B.C.-A.D. 18) gave us the following: "So long as you are secure you will count many friends; if your life becomes clouded you will be alone". Keep your days sunny and bright.

*You cannot teach a man anything*
*You can only help him discover it within himself!*
Galileo Galilei (1564-1642)

# One Hundred Sixteen

# The Fear of Success!

Talk to people about failure and success in the same breath and you'll get strange looks. After all these terms are actually opposites and yet...many will admit to a fear of failing while few of us understand the lesser-used concept of fearing to succeed. Therein lies my tale for today.

I was working with a group of financial consultants doing the second in a series of 7 workshops yesterday; this session was entitled "Goal-Setting and Success!". I asked the group to list their goals for the next year in the six most important areas of their lives...i.e. Physical, Mental, Spiritual, Family, Social and of course Financial. We also reviewed last year's goals. No one in the room had reached her/his financial objectives, albeit they all took the recession into account. After we filtered out the mundane and the usual "stuff" which accompanies failure, one word began to appear over and over again. They fully understood that they would never reach goals they did not feel were both *earned* and *deserved*. When asked why they felt undeserving, and thus failed to succeed the word finally came out. *Guilt!*

They all wanted to know how to get rid of this psychological mental block which affected their lives in a most negative way. We proceeded to explore where its power came from and how they carried it from the past into their current thinking and feeling. They volunteered that guilt is laid on them by parents, teachers, friends, peers, siblings, bosses, sales managers and religion. In other words, *anyone* wanting to control someone could press the guilt button installed by others from the past.

To get rid of the fear of success syndrome one has to let go of the reasons which were used originally to implant the bug deep in the subconscious, where it lay in wait to do its dirty work. This means no longer doing the "bad" things which trigger off the guilt feeling, thus paralyzing its owner. Going back to basics is a good way to start eliminating the problem. Also, reviewing and analyzing the feelings when they occur, thus rendering them helpless in the present...since their only power lay in dragging the past into the now.

Getting your act together as an intelligent, mature person begins with uprooting the guilt bug from its deep recesses of the mind, and tossing it out together with your past "sins" (?) ergo what people made you *feel* guilty over. After that, just do what you know is right when dealing with others and guilt will never come back, not matter how hard they try to hit your old button. God doesn't waste time judging us, being far too busy running this magnificent universe. We judge ourselves, too often based on *old messages* we received when susceptible to the influence of those around us. We must now repossess the power to judge, and use it based on current happenings.

Don't look back unless you want to drag your past into the present. Instead, listen to the advice of America's greatest philosopher, Emerson, as he wrote: *"Do the thing and you will have the Power"*.

*The proper function of man is to live, not to exist.*
*I shall not waste my time in trying to prolong them.*
*I shall use my time!*

Jack London (1876-1916)

# One Hundred Seventeen

# Born a Winner...Died a Whiner!

That's the epitaph we should be able to read on 4 out of 5 tombstones, if the truth be told. That's approximately the ratio of people who *make* things happen vs. allowing them to happen to them. If is half of the word l-if-e, and the losers go around *iffing* their way 50% of the time or more, blaming their lack of personal fulfillment in life to the "if only" syndrome. Instead of the tried and true method of living via "the next time", they bemoan their victim status, and continue to lead with their chins instead of learning to duck from their sobering experiences.

They remind me of the true story of Emmett Fox, eminent theologian and philosopher. On his maiden trip from England to New York City he went to his first cafeteria to have some lunch. He passed many counters full of food and drink...and sat down. He waited, waited and waited for someone to arrive and take his order. Finally, succumbing to the growls of his empty stomach he marched to the end of the line, observed the people helping themselves to the food they wanted, and followed suit. Shortly thereafter he enjoyed his first cafeteria-style lunch. He never forgot the lesson and used this story often from his pulpit.

We are all born into a life of abundance, with no personal limits imposed by nature on us. We can become *whatever* we want. Our gifts from our Creator are laid out in front of us for the taking and using. But we must dip into the bag of gifts, pull out the ones we intend to use and then go for it! Our gifts and talents will not jump out at us. Those of us who decide not to go after them will end up lost in self-pity. Self-pity is good to wallow in when we don't want to get our engine running and do something constructive with our lives. This engine will never stand still; if we don't use it rust begins to form and its gear slips into reverse. Just as cafeteria food will go bad if not used soon after it is displayed.

Charles Dickens (1812-1870) wrote: "Minds, like bodies, will often fall into a pimpled, ill-conditioned state from mere excess of comfort". Let's not get too comfortable. Auntie Mame put it very succinctly when she said: "Life is a banquet, and some poor sons-of-bitches are starving to death". The Reverend Emmett Fox chose not to be deprived of his portion once he understood the way the cafeterias of life work. Life delivers to both the winners and the whiners *exactly* what they order from it, so be very careful what you set your heart upon...for you'll surely attract it as a flame attracts a moth.

Winners visualize the future and the rewards of success, while whiners visualize the past with its penalties for failure, which they feel are deserved. "Born a winner...Lived...died a winner" is the way the epitaph *could* read, as

140

we take full control and responsibility for our destinies.

I have never forgotten what our great American statesman *Benjamin Franklin* once noted: "Some people die at twenty-five and aren't buried until they are seventy-five". Powerful stuff!

I sincerely believe that:

The time to grow is *now,*

The place to grow is *here,*

The person to grow is *you!*

As St. Paul put it so well..."When I was a child, I spoke as a child...I understood as a child...I thought as a child. When I became a man, I put away childish things."

# One Hundred Eighteen

# Flaunt Your M.B.A.

This is not a college degree...but rather one you earn by graduating from the school of hard knocks. This MBA stands for the Magnificent Being in Action you were born to be. This is what the preeminent psychologist Abraham Maslow (1908-1970) meant when he said that his studies of healthy people showed that less than 2% of us die having tasted our Greatness. This means that if I am addressing an audience of 1,000 people...980 of them would die without knowing they too could have lived a rich life, bold with meaning and fulfillment...ergo what Maslow describes as *self-actualized*.

Maslow also wrote: "a musician must make music, an artist must paint, a poet must write if he is to be ultimately at peace with himself." (Motivation and Personality...1954). My question now is: Is there a musician, artist or poet hiding inside you? If the answer is yes, what are you waiting for? If you are sublimating a strong desire to be something else than you are, peace of mind will elude you forever, and you will never know the joy of living up to your potential.

If you're stuck up to your chin in your old stories, climb out of the rut you're standing in. Move straight ahead, without so much as a glance backward *(the past)* and go for your heart's desire. I did not say your mind's desire (left brain). Go and follow your feelings; they may lead you to hitherto uncharted courses, full of new excitement. This will bring back the old enthusiasm with a vengeance, as you begin to do what you want, and not what those "others" in your life programmed you to do and to be.

Most of us go through life pushing the elevator button *after* someone else has already pushed it. As if that would make it come to your floor any faster. Self-actualized people not only do not need to push the button sheep-like, but will instead choose to walk up or down the stairs, maintaining their personal integrity by *doing* instead of *waiting* to be done unto. They fully understand that the universe is always creating, and they choose to follow the line of least resistance, i.e. create their lives. Self-actualized humans know that if you stop pedaling the bike you fall off...and that motion begets motion.

Magnificent Beings in Action make things *happen*. We all know the story of the two frogs who fell into a vat of milk. One of them...without an MBA, decided he could not get out and sank to the bottom of the vat, drowning. The other...a *two-percenter*, began to swim around the top of the milk at a fast pace. He knew that eventually the milk would turn to butter from his constant stirring. When it did, he simply climbed out...a winner with an M.B.A. diploma. When you run into some difficulty do you become a turnaround or a churnaround?

# One Hundred Nineteen

# The New Cultural Vocabulary

The past two generations have seen the growth of a new, multifaceted culture with its own unique vocabulary. The arts, music and dancing have taken new twists and turns hitherto never before attempted. Between breakdancing and the smashing of musical instruments as well as the use of pyrotechnics, loud decibels and smoke-bombs our senses are being assaulted on a new level. No wonder many teenagers have hearing problems. (Of course much of this comes from listening to *parents.*)

In just 40 years we've gone from Aristotle and Albeniz to Abdul (Paula), Balzac and Bartok to Bon Jovi and Black Crows, Confucius and Chopin to Chicago and Cher, Descartes and Dvorak to Dead (the Grateful), Epictitus and Elgar to Expose and Eagles, Flaubert and Faure to Firehouse and Factory, Goethe and Gounod to Guns 'n Roses and Genesis, Hawthorne and Holst to Heart, Ingersoll and Ives to Inxs, Kafka and Khachaturian to KISS, LaFontaine and Leoncavallo to Love & Rockets, Milton and Mozart to Madonna, Plato to Prince, Rabelais to Rolling Stones, and Yeats to YES!

We've gone from classical music and writing to noises and trash in several easy steps, as each decade heralded "new and improved" products and services. All this because today's boys and girls feel a greater need than ever before to express their individuality, since they have never been listened to *less* by their parents.

Mother Theresa, recipient of the Nobel Peace Prize, talks about a "spiritual deprivation" which erodes human values. I think she would certainly include the majority of today's alienated American youth in her appraisal. Subconsciously they want guidance and love from their parents...but they're afraid to put their needs on the line because there is no one there to listen! Parents too often are busily working several jobs to keep the American Dream from turning into a full nightmare. Also, they have to deal with their own insecurities...both as human beings and fathers and mothers. There is no blame, only sorrow. The once proud American eagle has landed, and will not fly again for a while.

People do not respect each other, as spiritual deprivation takes its toll among all segments of our nation. Politics, big business and education fail to develop healthy role-models for the young to want to emulate. Instead we read about the drug and sexual exploits of the sport heroes we admire.

Fortunately there are enough Americans interested in the revival of old, proven and traditional methods that have worked in the past and can continue into the *21st Century.*

U.S. President James Monroe said in his inaugural address on March 4, 1817 the following: "National honor is national property of the highest value". In "An Enemy of the People" (1882) the great European playwright Henrik Ibsen penned: "A community is like a ship; everyone ought to be prepared to take the helm". Are *you* ready to help guide the U.S.S. Constitution back home?

Make everyone in your life *important! Listen* to them. Since we only have one mouth and two eyes and two ears, let's learn to *see* and *hear* four times as much as *speak* in any one-on-one situation.

Also, *smille* often, and look people in the *eyes!*

That's what the new vocabulary, as well as the very old one is all about.

"Le plus ca change, le plus c'est la meme chose" i.e. "The more things change, the more they remain the same". From an Old French proverb.

**P.S.** I would like at this point to *categorically deny* that I intended a total prejudice against all modern music. I realize that while much of the sounds referred to earlier are inexcusable there are some fine tunes and lyrics worth hearing such as John Lennon's "Imagine" or some of the songs of conscience by "Woody's children". My concern is with the *lack of balance* between the "classics" and more modern themes.

# One Hundred Twenty

# Psychobabble

An office motto simply reads: "Little minds talk about people. Ordinary minds talk about events. Great minds talk about ideas!" I consider the first two groups as psychobabblers, since talking about people and events usually involves discussing the *past*. Ideas are of the *present* and peer into *the future*, a more realistic way to spend talk-time.

Today more than ever I hear conversations about what others are doing with their lives, and their attempts to cope with the daily frustrations resulting from the frenetic pace of the age we live in. The new systems to enhance life are literally mind-boggling (pun definitely *intended*). We hear words such as—transactional, primal, gestalt, psychocybernetics, meditation, transpersonal, reality, non-directive, analytic, bioenergetics, rational-emotive, rolfing and many other disciplines too numerous to list. It's enough to drive a sane person crazy. I have not even included therapies such as fire-walking and the beating of drums.

Therapists are becoming a larger part of the $700 billion pie which represents our annual health bill as a nation. And yet the results of all this new "self-nurturing" seems to have very little effect on the average populace. I think today's motto should be what Hillel "The Elder" (70 B.C.-A.D. 10) said: "If I am not for myself who is for me?..and being for my own self what am I? If not now, when?" I certainly believe in self-help, the accent being on the word *self*. But self means exactly that; no one else can undo for us what we did to ourselves. If we believe we are God's image individualized as humans then we do not need outside forces to bring us back. We just need to release our external stimuli, and go inside...seeking to plug back into the Universal Source. Sir James Hopwood Jeans, physicist and philosopher (1877-1946) in his famous Rede Lectures said: ..."the universe begins to look more like a great thought than like a great machine!"

What this means is that you can go back into Jung's collective unconscious and make contact with it, thus negating the need to fraternize with others in order to achieve self-understanding and acceptance. It's like coming home from a long and dangerous voyage, and continuing your life with renewed harmony. Einstein wrote it thus: "The simpler our picture of the external world, and the more facts it embraces, the stronger it reflects in our mind the harmony of the universe".

Once you let go of the ego trip most of us are on, life takes on new meaning. Instead of emotional immaturity leading to dysfunctional behavior, *self-love* and *harmony* will heal the past.

# One Hundred Twenty One
# Believing is Seeing

"Small is the number of them that see with their own eyes and feel with their own hearts." This quote from the as yet unmatched mental giant Albert Einstein, physicist and humanist, whose "relatively" simple formula E=Mc2 changed the way we see the world forever. The operant word repeated twice is *own*. He understood that we are mostly victims of outside conditioning, and therefore would, for the most part, see it from the external point of view...and we would *feel* based on what input we received from the forces nurturing us, positively or negatively.

Seeing with our own eyes and feeling with our own hearts would mean a return to our original innocence, the child-like quality we usually submerge when besieged by data received via our physical senses. If we can just get past what our eyes, ears, nose, taste and touch faculties bring into our lives, we would then find a world filled with intuition, insight, innate intelligence, and inspiration (Spirit within us). Einstein was a thinker, an original thinker who also believed that imagination is more important than knowledge. He took basic information already commonly accepted, turned it over to his inside eye to look over and re-evaluate. Then he recruited his formidable *imagination* supported by feeling to rethink and rework the old, thus producing new and original concepts for the benefit of mankind.

Another favorite quote of his was: "God does not play with dice". He understood the universe as an orderly process, with time and space working synergistically for ultimate good. He believed very strongly in contributing to the world, and not taking from it. His accomplishments notwithstanding he remained a very humble person, grateful for his intellectual gifts. I see his kindly eyes looking up at me whenever I sit by my desk, since his picture stares at me (under glass) from my desktop.

I like to think of him often because he is a great example of what a person can do with his/her life when it is *dedicated* to the furtherance of humanity. He fully understood another great law of the universe...that to give of himself is to truly receive. I'm sure he also intuited that what he was doing, others could also do...if they understood and believed they could. Since we are all part of one Universal Intelligence we could tap into it at will, once we eliminate the encumbrances we ourselves placed on top of it by our erroneous thinking and feeling. We've been told time and again that it is more blessed to give than to receive. This is true—but the giving must be from the real us, the original unadorned personality we were given at birth. That's when problems, frustrations and illnesses melt away from us, allowing us to dip into the *universal power* which makes things happen.

# One Hundred Twenty Two

# Right vs. Right!

Versus means against, contrary. When someone says to you "I'm right"....instead of "what's right?" that person is usually in the thinking/rational mode, wherein the ego plays an important role. It also means that *being* right is more important at that moment than *what* is right. Metaphorically speaking, it consists of putting fragile, emotion-laden eggs in a leaky basket, subject to vigorous shaking by anyone who disagrees. A dangerous practice to say the least, since it can lead to all forms of self-induced physical and mental ailments.

Being right is not necessarily doing right; there are no gray areas we can retreat into...mostly it is a matter of black or white. What's right will stand up a long time after who was right has bitten the dust of many yesteryears. There's a feeling attached to the *what* of right which can never become associated with the *who*. In an address given to The Young People's Society of Brooklyn in 1901...the inimitable Mark Twain said of right: "Always do right. This will gratify some people, and astonish the rest". Forty years earlier President Abraham Lincoln, during an address at Cooper Union (NYC) said: "Let us have faith that right makes might, and in that faith let us to the end dare to do our duty as we understand it".

Today right has taken on new meanings, fully divorced from previous interpretations. It's been said by many that the world will never be the "same" again...whatever that means. I can live with that. What I cannot condone is *repainting* the word right in different shades of gray, depending on the artist's need to restructure for his own purposes what is an unshakable truth. The business and political worlds both seem to benefit most from these new grays, as ethics are shed faster than dirty underwear.

Archie Bunker truly thinks he is right when he tells a friend that he is sure he has home insurance because he makes semi-annual payments *four times* a year. Most religions teach that theirs is the right one, chosen personally by God to represent our Creator on earth. I often wonder at how many rights we can accept, which differ from each other as day does night?

One good way to solve the Right vs. Right dilemma would be to go back into history and study the wisest utterances on the subject. Then, if what you find out feels right..i.e. you *intuit* its validity, go for it! You may find some interesting side effects. For example you may find out that you are your own worst enemy, and thus could easily become your best friend. All this takes is an unbiased look at your belief system (BS?). Then choose to change what needs changing, and reap the rewards of right living.

# One Hundred Twenty Three

# C.P.R.

CPR is regularly thought of as a life-saving technique, involving physical action. The CPR I refer to as a vignette title involves another life-saving technique, ergo our psychological side. CPR in this case stands for Contaminated Personality Reconstructed. Every time I do a workshop or seminar I run into people who are hurting on an emotional level. It seems as though each generation grows up with less ability to "cope" with life, and has to resort to *artificial means* to make it from day to day. Even the legal drugs are rampant, with over 50 million prescriptions annually.

There are literally dozens of disciplines preaching peace of mind, freeing the child within, growing into adulthood, etc...and yet the number of discontented is on the increase in all age groups. When Henry David Thoreau suggested that iconoclasts walk to the sound of a different drummer he was not referring to the drumming sessions for men which are the "in" thing these days. He understood full well that to go back into the past is no guarantee that the future would be any better. He wrote: "If you have built castles in the air, your work need not be lost; that is where they should be. Now put the foundations under them". Building castles in air is definitely *future* planning; putting foundations under them is current, or *present* thinking.

Research shows that only 4% of Americans will reach goals at age 65; they represent the high achievers who *make* things happen! The next 16% are busily watching the achievers do their thing...while the final 80% wonder what happened to the past 40 years.

Foundations are built one brick at a time, and it is their final cumulative result which can and will hold up edifices, including castles. This reminds me of the tale of a father and son walking on a very dark night in a cavern, carrying a single lit candle between them. The young boy, fearing for his life begged his father to turn back...since, as he put it: "The candle lights but for a short distance". His father wisely replied: "We will move ahead—as we proceed forward the candlelight will continue to show the way. One short step at a time will do it".

Reconstructing a contaminated personality is possible once we accept and understand our Mental Power. To quote the philanthropist J.C. Penney: "No man (person) need live a minute longer as he is, because the Creator endowed him with ability to change himself". Science has discovered that within each atom of our body is a center of light. Uncover your light, and use it to move forward...one step at a time, and *get rid* of the candle.

# One Hundred Twenty Four

# Do You Have An NBA?

Most people I encounter daily, whether at work or at play possess what I call an NBA...Negative Belief Attitude. They go around waiting for Murphy's Law to take effect...ergo if anything can go wrong it will! And then when that happens, they contentedly say "I knew it!" as they fulfill yet another negative prophecy. This NBA is not earned in college but in the school of hard knocks known as Life. Unlike school, however, we can change our grades completely as we change our beliefs which led to the low scores originally.

As I look over Abraham Maslow's Hierarchy of Needs I notice that most of us seem to be stuck somewhere between the third and fourth rung from the bottom of his pyramid (ladder?). It's as if we were caught in the act of climbing toward the top...i.e. *self-actualization,* but one foot became stuck on the second rung and the other foot is on the third rung, also trapped permanently by crazy glue. We can see the top of the pyramid but cannot reach it. And so we go through life, frustrated and bitter because we can't have what is within our sight. (Just like TV and its ads for things many of us cannot afford).

The steps our feet are bonded to represent our Love and Belonging needs, our *Esteem* needs. We want to be accepted, belong, gain approval and recognition...and be competent. And the glue holding us back from moving upward is our outdated Be-System...our antiquated B.S. (Yes, BullShit!) The trick here is to begin with self-acceptance, self-approval, self-recognition, and the feeling of self-competence...backed by unshakable belief in our potential.

A non-judgmental philosophy will really help at this point in life...with judgment to be withheld from both yourself and the others...something far easier *written* than done. By reviewing daily the number of times you judge yourself and others you can begin to eliminate this painful mental block wherein you punish yourself for the guilt associated with it. This will free you from the third and fourth steps, and you can begin the upward climb once again on Maslow's personal success pyramid.

The next need we have is *cognitive.* It includes a quest for knowledge, understanding and a desire for further exploration. The step above this one brings to fruition our *aesthetic need,* i.e. for symmetry, order and beauty. Finally, graduation day...as we reach the pinnacle, finding self-fulfillment and realizing our full human potential.

Now our physical needs are taken care of; also our requirements for safety and security. We belong to some peer groups and we begin to receive and accept approval and recognition from them. As our esteem grows we understand more and begin to appreciate the beauty all around us. Finally, *self-actualization* allows us to be us, as we reshape our Future. Agathon the Greek wrote 24 centuries ago: "This only is denied to God: the power to undo the past". Forget the past and begin enjoying the present.

Become a problem-solver, and start with yours. Accept yourself as you *are*, subject to changes you decide on ... no one else. Remember that you are a Unique Creation of Universal intelligence. Make the most of yourself ...that's all life requires of you. Become the best you, and you will attract the best in others.

# One Hundred Twenty Five

# Life is a Boomerang

What you send out...comes back—in one form or another. For example, if you send out anger vibes one of two things is bound to happen. First, the object of your anger may elect to catch it, boomerang it back to you, then with *interest* added to it. Or, if the receiver of your p.o. attitude decides not to receive, and ducks instead your feeling will automatically boomerang back to you...and then *you'll* be adding the interest to it, thus increasing its negative, destructive power. A classic case of lose-lose mentality.

If you telegraph a grudge or judgment (*grudgement*) against another human, you stand a good chance of "eating your words", since universal law dictates that "what you give out, will be measured back to you...with interest". The perfect reason to make sure your words are properly sugared and spiced, so that they are easily digestible.

Unconditional love is the answer, if boomeranging is to become a game with you...and not a punishment. I recently heard a woman at my favorite bagel emporium say the following to her young son: "Of course I love you unconditionally...as long as you do exactly as I say!"

The trick is to learn to control the boomerang. Once you understand its aerodynamics you can predict the immediate future, something 4 out of 5 people do not possess to any measurable degree. Healthy self-control comes as a result of using empathy, compassion and genuine concern for others.

The boomerang effect also works on the human mind through the not always subtle messages coming over the omnipresent TV tube. This 24-hour a day purveyor of mental garbage sends out its negative output to nearly-hypnotized minds no longer able to discern between fact and fiction. The result...*the boomerang,* wherein people tend to throw back into the world what they have been digesting subliminally. I find, to my dismay that too many young minds today are excellent at rote-learning, but do little thinking. To make things worse, the latest data gathered by dozens of concerned organizations tell us that once they leave school, 3 out of 5 Americans *never again* read a book...while the other 2/5 consume only 1 book per year. The same research shows that almost 40% of the American public is functionally illiterate or as we now call them...*dysfunctional.*

If you watch violence constantly, violence will become a part of your life, since our "feeling" (right) brain absorbs it without objective judgment. According to the Center for Continuing Education at the Australian National University, "our usual processes of thinking and discernment are semi-functional at best" when we watch television. A very scary report.

# One Hundred Twenty Six

# UPS Calling

Are you waiting for the UPS truck to deliver something to you right now? The majority of us would have to say no...and yet, when one psychologist asked 3,000 people what they were waiting for, fully 93% replied: "I'm waiting for something to happen!" If you didn't put in your order for a package you'll sit and wait forever. And this is what 2790 people out of 3000 are quite willing to do. What are *you* sending out which will require a response? If you put a kettle of water on a stove and wait for it to boil you'll turn into a skeleton before you hear the whistle which signals the water is ready for pouring. *Unless* you turn the power source on under the kettle.

Life moves on whether *you* decide to participate or not. Non-active, or passive participation uses up exactly the same amount of time. Doesn't it make sense to use it up constructively? If you're going to live to age 80 you have less than 7,000 days to insure your success. The first 20 years are used to acquire knowledge necessary to make the other 60 fruitful. That leaves 3,120 weeks or 21,915 days. Knock off 1/3 of that time, i.e. 20 years for sleeping, and you're down to only 14,610 days to produce and achieve.

Now, erase your weekends from the altered total; this will cost you 6,240 days...leaving you with a new low of 8,370. We now come to legal holidays, vacations and sick leave. These add up to an average of 1,800 days...leaving you with a net of only 6,570 days in which to leave your mark on this planet. That is, if you live to be 80. Now subtract your current age from 80 and eliminate the first 20 years of your life (your "learning" vs. "earning" time) and you'll know how many years you have left. You can now choose to wait for the grim reaper to whisk you away...or you can decide to make life so important and valuable that you will live it to the fullest, oblivious of mortality statistics. After all, for each person dying at age 60 someone must live to 100 in order to make the average (80) work.

Longevity involves action, not waiting. George Burns is already contracted to do the London Palladium at age 100. What a wonderful attitude he has. Should he miss the 100 mark, it won't be by much. The lesson? Set your goals high, so that even failure to reach them will leave you on a better level of personal achievement than reaching low goals. The Koran says: "He deserves Paradise who makes his companions laugh." George Burns' future is thus assured...The great artist Andy Warhol has this to add: "They always say that time changes things, but you actually have to change them yourself." *Change yourself first* and time will take on a new dimension in your life.

# One Hundred Twenty Seven

# Singles, The Beaten Generation

It's been exactly 10 years since I had done my last singles talk, so I was partially unprepared for what I heard and saw. A decade ago I spoke in front of hundreds of singles, who were for the most part high on life. Yesterday, I met with a group in which many had a "beaten" look and attitude about them. I detected quite a few desperate, haunting looks as they (*a high majority were women*) walked around exchanging bad-luck stories of dates which proved to be disappointing. I had to ask myself what their dates thought of them, and where the blame *really* lies.

Looking over the monthly schedule of events for this singles organization, I found activities planned for them for fully 26 days. And yet, the only event which was designed specifically to help them eliminate connecting with the wrong people was my talk entitled: "How to Attract & Develop a Loving Relationship". All the other times were designed to help singles have *fun*! No wonder many of them are ready to throw in the towel, and settle for second or third best...meaning they will surely be single again in the future.

To make sure my material was original, I put together the acronym *singles life*, using each letter as a mnemonic device. I want to share with you what I told them, since the ideas shared with this group will work for all of us. After all, even singles are parents, children, in-laws, siblings and co-workers. Therefore any people skills I was discussing will work with contacts other than dates. Now for the acronym Singles Life.

S- stands for *sincerity* in all relationships, including children, friends and relatives.

I- represents our strongest human emotional need...to feel *important.* This means make others feel more important, and they will want to be with you as often as possible. I is also the beginning of *Individual*, which each of us must maintain for good mental health.

N- is for *Networking*. I explained the 7 deadly sins of non-productive networking.

G- for the "biggie"...*Guilt,* and how to eliminate it. Also, *Goals*, and how to attain them.

L- begins the word *love*...which we all want, but feel unworthy to receive. Also, *loyalty* to family and principles.

E- *Enthusiasm*...allow the God within to come out and play!

S- for *Selling* yourself and your ideas to others.

L- Learn to *laugh*, and don't take life too seriously.

I- for using more Intuition, Insight, Inspiration and Imagination in relationships.

F- make *Friends* First, lovers later (if it feels right).

E- for *excellence* in all you attempt...and *Ethics*.

I elaborated for one hour on the above subject headings and received excellent feedback from the group.

I learned that night that on Long Island there are over *ten single women* for every male... and yet, you can't find many of the men at the programs designed for singles. What's needed is a sales course for single men, to teach them to sell themselves and their ideas to other singles. Well, I'm ready to teach when they come out of the woodwork.

# One Hundred Twenty Eight

# A Review of Self-Esteem

The cover of Newsweek Magazine tells the readers that the main article in that issue is dedicated to Self-Esteem. True to its word it devotes a full 7 pages to that all-important topic. I'll capsulize some of its major findings. First, when asked what were the most important factors in motivation with regards to working hard and succeeding...a high majority (89%) of those polled agreed that Self-Esteem (the way people feel about themselves) was very important. When asked if too much time and effort is spent on self-esteem, fully 63% felt that the time and effort spent was worthwhile.

What struck me as strange were the answers to another question. When asked "Who would you say has low self-esteem?" 10% of those responding said: "Me, personally". They also said that "other relatives" having low self-esteem numbered 50%. There seems to be a *denial factor* at work here, when they can see others as having 5X as much low self-esteem as themselves. My own research...not done by telephone with strangers...shows that well over 80% of Americans need to improve their self-image, or self-worth.

When asked which situations would make them feel bad about themselves here were the answers, from the worst scenario down:

1- Not able to pay bills
2- Having an abortion
3- Getting divorced...or doing something immoral
4- Losing your job...or disobeying God
5- Being noticeably overweight
6- Doing something embarrassing in public
7- Being criticized by someone you admire

Interestingly enough only doing something immoral, which is disobeying God (as we have been taught) has to do with self-esteem. The remaining problems mentioned have more to do with others, and *their esteem of you*. This means letting the opinions of *others* decide how you are going to feel. Not very easy to live with, I'm afraid. The idea is to strengthen our own self-feelings, so that we can survive an assault by well-meaning (?) friends, relatives or associates.

This means a reevaluation of what is most important *to you*. If your self opinion matches that of those around you so much the better. If they clash, find a new set of nurturing relationships, who are not so quick to judge you, and accept you...fat thighs, jug ears, harelip and all. People who judge others are only reflecting their own flaws...and need much work on their own self-esteem. Oscar Wilde once said: "To love oneself is the beginning of a lifelong romance". What a wonderfully positive statement. On the negative side we accept the genius of Leo Tolstoy, who wrote: "I am always with myself, and it is I who am my tormentor". Let's stop tormenting ourselves as of now!

You can't always control what you're thinking, but you can always control how you will *act!*   Develop a Positive Mental Attitude by the use of daily affirmations...based on what you want to become and not what you are now.

William Ernest Henley who lived from 1849 to 1903 wrote: "I am the master of my fate: I am the captain of my ship!" Like a ship's captain, know where you're headed as your final destination, but look ahead only 50 yards at a time.  If you take care of the immediate you'll reach your goal without trial, trauma, or tribulation.  And watch your *self-esteem* grow as you travel through life in full command of your ship.

# One Hundred Twenty Nine
# The G-Spot, An Update!

Recently, when giving a lecture I had to use the letter G as part of the presentation. This letter represented one of the major problems most of us have to contend with on a daily basis. In order to pull the word out of my audience I mentioned that the letter began a word which is most often thought of by both Jews and Catholics...coming from totally different religions. With almost a roar the room exploded with the word—*Guilt!* Not even a nanosecond went by between the question and the answer. Guilt, the great controller and manipulator of our lives, once again reared its ugly head.

If we took away the power of the clergy to forgive, and took it back...most religious edifices would quickly crumble and decay from lack of use. Without the ability to use (misuse) guilt via the forgiveness route, organized religion would have to find new ways to earn a living. Since they teach us that we are made in God's image, it stands to reason that we can bypass them and do the forgiving on our own, drawing the strength to free ourselves of guilt from our *inner divinity*. 'Physician heal thyself' could be changed to "sinner forgive thyself", ergo heal spiritually, automatically dissolving all past and present guilt.

Guilt also comes in handy when parents, teachers, spouses, siblings, bosses, managers, friends and lovers want to *control* others. Once they have found a weak spot in our character, they will use a cattle prod to make us jump at their command. I have chosen to give up guilt as a bad job, and I have relegated it to my stormy and often erratic past...where it belongs.

I believe feelings of guilt are constructive only when used to eliminate wrong actions toward other people, and that only I should use it as a means to a greater and healthier self-image. If I continue to hurt someone (on purpose) guilt can and should come into my life to wreak physical and mental havoc, until I stop the destructive behavior. Many times when I want to say or do something negative a small voice inside my head quickly says: *"you can't do that!"*...and I stop in my tracks. I usually end up laughing, which certainly beats pouting or resisting the *"invice"* (advice from within). I find this an excellent way to keep my side of relationships going the way I want them to.

Shakespeare tells us of a bad byproduct of guilt, when he writes in Henry VI: "Suspicion always haunts the guilty mind; The thief doth fear each bush an officer". How right he is, as we transfer our guilt into those around us, infecting them with the same germ without their knowledge. If we don't trust ourselves it is difficult to trust others, since we see them as being the same as we.

I believe that as we diminish our guilts our self-esteem will grow in direct opposite proportion. The less guilt to feel bad about, the more we have to feel good about in ourselves.

Success in life is the result of Self-Confidence married to Positive Expectancy. But you must live in the *now*. Don't live in the past or in the future...the present requires your full attention.

I honestly believe that *today is the best day of your life!* Believe it, and make it so. The power is in you. Just go ahead with your life, and miss the mark no more (i.e. sin). With no sin, Guilt will melt away and bother you no more.

# One Hundred Thirty

# Walk Your Talk!

To talk less and do more was advice given to me by my father many years ago. I believe that he also meant that when you did talk, make sure your actions followed your words...thus "Walk Your Talk!", Too many of us are locked into a "say one thing and do another" philosophy, thereby confusing our mind's circuitry and lowering its ultimate productivity.

"Change your thoughts an change your life" still holds true, but this is probably easier said than done. Sometimes our bodies learn the lessons of life faster than our minds do. For example, it only takes one exposure of a finger on a hot stove to learn caution when approaching warm/hot objects. And yet we can get burned emotionally many times, and still not learn the lessons involved. It takes a streak of masochism to continue to do the things that hurt us. One of the dictionary definitions of masochism is: "Pleasure in being abused or dominated. A suffering."

If you want to continue to suffer, don't bother to read on. However, if you're bound to give up your old stories...which generally are nothing but dusty old archives of human misery, you can follow along as I develop a theme to help frame a better future than the past has been. First understand that living in the past R.O.B.S. (Reliving Old Belief System) your future of all creativity. Hence, you must begin by digging into your photographic mind and remove all the negatives stored therein.

If you refuse to enjoy today because of what happened all those yester-days, you're doomed to repeat them! Remember that past mistakes do not make you special. Remembering that you're made in God's image does make you special...and that's what you must learn to concentrate on. *Relearn* because you lost that feeling somewhere along life's journey if it is not working for you now.

I know that you're not part of the "lookers-shoppers" out there who buy book after book on personal development and self-help...then proceed to *blame the books* when things don't change as they hoped. Intelligent people realize that these books only confirm what they already intuited...that they *already have* all the know-how necessary for happy living, and need only to put the ideas to work. The books then become tools designed to reinforce the ancient knowledge we all possess at birth. My personal library of over 400 books shows me different ways to look at old concepts and to bring them into the 21st Century (I like to look ahead). Choose what you want guiding your thoughts, then *walk your talk*, since actions do speak louder than mere words.

# One Hundred Thirty One

# The Unbionic Man

Most of us do not have the luxury of being rebuilt by our scientists once our parts begin to go. They can replace limbs and give us plastic hearts...but nothing can improve on the human body, received at birth. Through the mind it has retained the original power of life and death. I have almost ninety books on holistic health, proving we have the ability to make or break our bodies, *one cell at a time*. The instantaneous healings recorded by the medical profession now run in the thousands...and include tumors, cancers and even the most dreaded disease of all, AIDS.

Born as we all were full of potentialities we have to wonder why most of us are dragged through life silently screaming with rage at our unhappy fates. Surely our Creator had something better in mind for us. Unfortunately it is *our interference* with the natural order of things which make for a mediocre or at best, an average life. Read any religious work and you'll find references to our being in charge of this world...and that only *good* should be our individual lot. Where then did we lose the message?

We lost it when we decided to reinvent the rules of the universe, using our ego for our guidelines. When we began to think and believe that *we* were in charge the troubles began. We stopped dipping into the right brain hemisphere, where our intuition, insight, inspiration and imagination are waiting to be used for our common good. Instead we turn to the left side where our rational, linear and analytical hemisphere tells us we are in full charge, and need not bother with our gifts inherited via the creation route. The *think vs. feel* battle continues to ravage our mental and physical health, as the ego strives to separate us from Universal Intelligence. Our life choices become very simple as Left seeks to control Right. Here are some examples of the self-destruct mission many of us are on:

We would rather...win (L) than heal(R)...cry than laugh...judge than accept...be right than happy...fearful than loving. We would also rather suffer than submit...hurt than yield...have conflict than peace of mind...

Why would we choose this self-destruction instead of the "good life" promised in all philosophical and religious works? Because we continue to replay our old mental tapes, the ones telling us we'll burn in hell...that everything we do is being written down (or computerized now)...that we were born in sin...that we are the cause of our parents' problems, and mostly that *we are unworthy* and will never amount to anything. Using guilt as a manipulative tool those who would nurture us too often annihilate our Self-Esteem...the one we all had in great abundance when we first entered this world.

We must review *(once only)* those old tapes and have the courage to discard the outdated messages, which have nothing in common with our current thinking and feeling. Only then will we be able to go through life not worrying about our body parts breaking down. A plastic heart will give *plastic love!*

Fix your mind on a *purpose* for your life and observe the physical change in you. Having a reason above and beyond the mundane "earning a living syndrome" will net you new vigor and vitality as you go about fulfilling your new dream.

Mary Wollstonecraft Shelley...(1797-1851) suggested the following idea: "Nothing contributes so much in tranquilizing the mind as a steady purpose--a point on which the soul may fix its intellectual eye".

# Mark Twain...21st Century Man

"Oh East is East, and West is West, and never the twain shall meet," (Rudyard Kipling...1865-1936). I believe Rudyard Kipling probably did meet Mark Twain since they were contemporaries (1835-1919). Mark Twain, the great satirist once wrote: "Deep down in his heart no man much respects himself". Metaphorically speaking, let us think of Kipling's East and West as our left and right brains, and then add the fact that most of us do not use them correctly as one unit. As a result most of us walk around burdened with a poor image of ourselves.

An analogy comes to mind. Take a balloon filled with helium and attach dozens of strings tied to cement cubes at its base. Place it in a deep pool and watch it sink. Begin cutting the strings one at a time and eventually the balloon will begin to rise to the top. Once free of all the strings it will soar into the atmosphere, thus fulfilling its destiny as a helium balloon. The same holds true of people. The cement cubes are the *old guilts* and *angers*...firmly anchored to our subconscious, causing us to stay well below our normal level of accomplishment. In order to soar and fulfill our role as God's chosen heirs of the planet we must cut the cords tying us to our spotted past.

The steps we need to take for this transformation include an attitude of non-resistance to healthful change, forgiveness of all involved in our lives and releasing the feelings which caused the original problems to persist. To begin we must accept only those ideas which conform to the person we *want to become,* rather than the one we have been. Forgiveness becomes easier to manage once we understand that every person is out there doing the best s/he can...based on her/his current level of psychological and emotional maturity *(or lack thereof)*. The last step involves the emotional release of old feelings associated with the person or event when it occurred.

The "an eye for an eye" or a "tooth for a tooth" philosophy simply does not work. All you end up with are two angry blind or toothless people instead of one, thus compounding the original trouble. Letting go of revenge thoughts shows at least one of you is growing as a human(e) being.

The finest example of non-resistance to change is *water*. Depending on the conditions surrounding it, water will glide over, under, around and through objects with consummate ease, without disturbing the original terrain. When the weather is very cold, water will easily turn into ice. When boiling it will evaporate and release incredible energy, again effortlessly. Our minds can become as calm as water and as powerful as the gigantic turbines it spins, once we *let go,* and *let it happen.*

# One Hundred Thirty Three

## Life...The Best School!

Last night I had one of my rare headaches. Since I couldn't get to my chiropractor for quick relief I relied on the only pills I ever take, aspirins. In order not to wake up my wife I removed two capsules from the Nuprin plastic bottle by the reflection of the night light...and downed them with water. The next morning I felt better. When I told my wife about it at the breakfast table she burst out laughing. It seems I had taken two Amoxycillin (improved Penicillin) instead of Nuprin; they are to be used for infections (not headaches). Because I believed they were aspirins they acted on my system as aspirins and relieved the headache. Also, I did not get an infection all day. Ah, the wonderful power of placebos.

Once again I was reminded that the mind controls the body; not the other way around, as was believed for many centuries. For some of us, attempting to re-educate the mind is like trying to teach a jackass to dance. You'll end up wasting your time and frustrating the hell out of the jackass. Since I believe that many headaches are caused by *infectious negativity* perhaps my subconscious knew what it was doing when it picked the capsules which cure *infections*.

Life and its myriad experiences teaches the best outside lessons when we pay attention. Pay is the right word, because if we don't pay now (attention to the immediate problem) we will pay for the solution many times over. Sort of like taking Vitamin C to prevent colds. People who chronically complain that life has dealt them a rotten hand are playing in the wrong card game. I like to think that we were all born with a stack of aces, and then proceed to waste them by playing against twos and threes. If your hand is "rotten" it's because you've allowed "crap 'n crud" to get into your thinking, and it spilled over into your aces.

"Just who do you think you are?" is a phrase I remember hearing often during my teens. Also, "You're getting too big for your britches!" Perhaps I spilled over my britches because I had allowed by thinking brain to land down there, far away from its original source of creation. As for who I think I am, I know I am an extension of Universal Intelligence, and can tap into it at will...as I still my outer senses. This will reveal and reinforce the fact that my greatest inheritance lies within me, waiting for me to claim it in full.

I never fail to mention in my keynoters and seminars that as we are made in God's image we can ask for *anything* and *get it*...as long as it does not harm or take from anyone else. The urge to continually multiply is the strongest in the universe, and you can see the evidence daily as you look around at nature's bounty. If you think of the contents in your medicine cabinet as the lessons you are learning outside of yourself, and believe in a

Creator (placebo) you can proceed to seal the cabinet door for you'll never have to dig in there again. You will now be privy to the wisdom of the ages as you converse with your collective unconscious, the source of it all.

Do with your life what Eleanor Roosevelt, one of the great First Ladies of America did with hers. Her philosophy was simple: "I could not at any age be content to take my place in a corner by the fireside and simply look on. Life was meant to be lived. One must never, for whatever reason, turn one's back on life". When one is busy doing instead of bitching, sickness cannot grab a hold and loses any grip it might have had in the past. Optimism has been proven to be a powerful opiate. Use it as often as needed; you cannot overdose on it.

# One hundred Thirty Four

# Wherever I Go...I Already Am!

Since I have to take me along wherever I go, I decided to make sure I have a strong personal relationship with me. So I made friends with myself, a feat which took decades to successfully perform. Why? Because for years I was not easy to get along with. In fact, if I could I would have escaped from myself many times. The main reason for this is that what I *wanted* and what I felt I *deserved* were in constant conflict. Thinking and feeling were always at odds, screwing up a good portion of my life. I'm sure many of my readers fully understand the conflict which raged inside me.

In order to make peace with myself I had to match my thoughts with my feelings, thus forming a permanent alliance between the two previously warring factions. I believe it's working. I know, because earlier this week I had proof of it once again. I was shopping at my favorite CVS and sauntering in the aisles, watching people mesmerized by the plethora of color and variety displayed on the shelves. As I breezed through the health section I noted several aisles filled with miracle drugs whose sole "raison d'aitre" was to help alleviate the discomforts of Coughs...Colds...and Conditions. I mean *hundreds of promises* locked away in little jars, boxes, liquids and pills. If that store depended on my purchasing these items it would have to go into bankruptcy.

Once I understood the direct relationship between mental confusion and physical ills manifesting from the neck up I had the option of staying with the sufferers or getting away from them. I chose not to remain a victim. Instead I opted for mental cooperation and equilibrium. The journey I took inward is still going on; I expect it to last until I draw my final breath. On the road inside my head I found many old enemies, ready to trip me up at any time, thus confusing my life once more. Ergo the return of the colds 'n coughs. These enemies include unresolved conflicts, angers, hatred, thoughts of revenge and frustrations.

In order to rid myself of these obstacles to good health I used a "dustbuster" vacuum cleaner called *rational behavior.* I now use it nightly just before going to bed. I think and feel my way out of the clutter, ending up with a clean slate nightly. I know three ways to handle any disturbance in my life. One, I can accept it without judgement. Two, I can reject it as unreasonable. Finally and most important I can forgive th doer of the deed as well as the receiver (me)...and let go of the feelings which can manifest as ill health. Norman Cousins tells us in "Head First": "I have learned that life is an adventure in forgiveness". He also wrote: "The surest way to intensify an illness is to blame oneself or the Deity". Reader, *heal thyself!*

165

# One Hundred Thirty Five

# The Lost Instructions

Most new things come with instructions. Tools, games, toys, even recipes for gourmet foods. Instructions: an outline or manual of technical procedure (Webster's Collegiate Dictionary). Seems to me that there is one outdated lexicon. The most important definition has been left out, ergo that of human procedure. We seem to have lost the instructions which come with every new baby, procedures automatically imprinted in the newborn's mind. It only takes a careful look into the eyes of the child to read the following guidelines:

1- I am made in the image of *God*.

2- My main source of nourishment is *Love*.

3- I have *Intuitive* knowledge of the entire human race.

4- I have *unlimited* Human Potential.

"Please do not fold, spindle or mutilate me in any way, physically, mentally or spiritually. This is a user-friendly universe."

Instead of carefully following directions, parents too often permutate them to suit their own neurotic needs. In the final analysis neurotics beget neurotics, who will beget neurotics, unless someone breaks the chain and helps normalize the next generation.

Sometimes I think parents-to-be need to pass a written as well as oral exam, designed to insure that they can follow the simple instructions which come at the birth of their children. Teenagers who become pregnant are hardly ready for motherhood, and the teenagers who father them don't begin to understand the awesome responsibility which accompanies the birth of a new child. Drug and alcohol addicts of all ages cannot follow the guidelines mentioned above; they're far too busy fulfilling their own lack of self-esteem.

Oscar Wilde (1854-1900) wrote exactly a century ago in "The Picture of Dorian Gray" the following: "Children begin by loving their parents; as they grow older they judge them; sometimes they forgive them". I believe that parenting is *the most difficult job* anyone can ever undertake. A car mechanic needs a license to prove his/her expertise. So do electricians, plumbers and even carpenters. Parents only need the ability to procreate, same as the animal kingdom.

JFK once said: "Every American ought to have the right to be treated...as one would wish his children to be treated. This is not the case". (June 11, 1963) TV address on civil rights. Why is it that we always think others should treat our children any better than we as parents generally do?

If the National PTA is right, and parents give 8 *negative strokes* for each *positive* their children receive from them, it is no wonder each generation is prone to more crimes committed at younger ages. The changes must begin with the *parents*.

# One Hundred Thirty Six

## Cosmos, 10 Years Later

Carl Sagan, astronomer emeritus wrote a book in the early '80s titled "Cosmos". He had already written a dozen books plus 400 scientific and popular articles, and in 1978 received the Pulitzer Prize for literature. Whenever my ego threatens to get out of control, or move from a back burner in my mind to a front one I pick up Carl's magnificent contribution to the universe. As I read that there are some 100 billion galaxies each containing on the average 100 billion stars, my self-indulgent ego slides back into its rightful place, i.e. the back of my own mental universe.

Therefore I cannot even begin to think of this limitless creation being run so efficiently without a *helmsman steering it.* Again and again I am reminded of the words uttered by Vincent van Gogh, "peintre extraordinaire": "I have...a terrible need...shall I say the word?...of religion. Then I go out at night and paint the stars". He understood religion as a communion with the force behind the movement of the galaxies as he saw them, albeit in a most primitive way. The book Cosmos has hundreds of pictures in it which the mind of van Gogh could not even hint at, much less attempt to paint.

And yet, to know that we are unraveling the secrets of the universe at breakneck pace makes me feel humble, since a mere 3-pound mass of gray matter is the tool used. That's when my ego shrinks back to its proper size and retreats from my current thoughts. Thus chastised, I can go back to enjoy the marvels of infinite variety as visual proof of a universal architect. Later, as I listen to a favorite Mozart symphony I am also reminded that Universal Intelligence immortalized the composer by using him as a conduit for unforgettable musical creations.

I would not trade my brain for all the computers in the world, which cannot *think, feel or create.* Whether I look into the night sky, or listen to great music, or read a classic work, my mind thinks, my heart feels and my intelligence creates new inroads into old ideas. The book this vignette is printed on is made basically from a tree, once again showing the synchronicity and *interconnection of all things.* The idea that the universe is one Grand Thought has been acceptable for a long period of time.

From the great physicist James H. Jeans (1877-1946) we read in "The Mysterious Universe"—1930: "...From the intrinsic evidence of his creation, the Great Architect of the Universe now appears as a *pure mathematician*". Add to this what the finest mind to date, Albert Einstein, has to say in his "Physics and Reality" published in 1936: "The whole of science is nothing more than a refinement of everyday thinking". This means that you and I both have a *scientist* or *artist* hiding in the recesses of our minds.

# One Hundred Thirty Seven

## Scientist or Artist?

Two cannibals are having lunch in deepest Africa, while exchanging their most personal thoughts as life-long friends do. Suddenly one turns to the other and says: "You know, I really hate my mother-in-law". "That's all right", replies his friend. *"Just eat the vegetables."* My question is: are you busily chewing things over and over again in your mind—things which you *hate*? To put it another way...are you wasting quality think-time on previously painful experiences? If the answer is yes, may I admonish you eat the "vegetables" only, thus staying in the immediate present, which is the only time frame you have any degree of control over.

My title reads Scientist or Artist? because, as Napoleon the First (1769-1821) once said: "Every French soldier carries a marshal's baton in his knapsack". While on the isle of St. Helena he also remarked: "My maxim was, *la carriere est ouverte aux talents,* (the tools to him that can handle them) without distinction of birth or fortune". He understood very well that we are all born with talents restricted only by our own thinking! Therefore we all have within us the potential for becoming world class scientist (left-brain) or artist (right brain), depending on whether we use *thinking* or *feeling* most predominantly in our quest for personal success and happiness.

When we continue to occupy our minds with graffiti gathered throughout the years, it leaves little room for growth. Eating the vegetables only allows us to bring new ideas to the surface, thus displacing the old permanently. This will result in recapturing control of our destiny.

When you put the brakes on subtractive living, ergo things which don't make you feel good about yourself...you invite their opposite, or "living plus". Reminds me of the bumper sticker I saw recently which espouses the idea perfectly. It read: *"God already made my day!"* Don't be like Alice in Wonderland, who kept on running just to keep in place. Standing still in the race of life is going backwards, since the mind never rests. It either moves forward and grows or lives in the past and shrinks down to a minuscule size, the end product of its repeated failures.

Instead, failure can be turned into success by a continuing transfer of *enthusiasm*. Diseases are not the only things which can be passed along; enthusiasm is also very contagious. But like vitamin C it must be renewed daily in order to have a lasting effect. Spiritual poverty benefits no one, whereas enrichment of the soul touches everyone.

In proverbs we read: "He that troubleth his own house shall inherit the wind" (11:29). If you read "house" as our own mind, the meaning will become very clear. Let's not get too winded.

# One Hundred Thirty Eight _____

# Clone the Clone!

It's been said that until age 20 we continually worry about what others think of us. After 40, we no longer care what they think of us...and once we pass 60 we discover, with dismay, that they *never really thought about us at all!* If this is true why do youngsters mimic and mirror the styles, clothes and hairdos of their peers? Why do they chance looking ridiculous in the eyes of the non-participants? Because they think they're being original...thus above and beyond the pressure of their contemporaries.

Evidences of a low self-esteem abound when observing these "nouveau", hormone-active adolescents. They'll wear different clothes, sneakers, hair styles, as long as their "difference" is equal to the difference of those they befriend and "hang around" with (my teenager's phrase). Thus they are unlike the others, i.e. the unacceptables. Dorks don't dress like dweebs, dweebs don't ape jocks, scrubs don't primp like preps, nerds hopefully need glasses. Sometimes dirtbags can be mistaken for lowlifes, and so on. But they do dress alike within the caste system they are loyal to. The only thing I've noticed they all have in common is that none of the various groups initiate original thinking. Thus, they fail to use the one constant which they inherited at birth...their *innate intelligence,* with its immeasurable parameters.

Due to the hi-tech world we now live in thinking has been relegated to the ignoble position of "non grata", Latin for non-acceptable. Only a minority, those destined for greatness continue to use their brains for something better than a hat rack. That's why less tan 5% become the *movers and shakers* as they choose *not* to follow the herd, and decide instead to use what we all inherited at birth in equal amounts. Clones following clones reinforce the old adage "misery loves company". Uniqueness is one of the great gifts the Universal Source has bestowed upon us. Not to make the best use of this positive quality means remaining average, in other words dull! Today's kids may be smarter than ever, but definitely not *wiser.* When it comes to common sense it is practically non-existent. Facts, figures and friends form the bulk of the collection amassed in the high school years. Ethics, values, and skills for dealing with people are left in a dust-heap of forgotten times.

Almost two centuries ago the writer Charles Caleb Colton gave us this philosophical gem: "Imitation is the sincerest form of flattery". That might have worked when we had legitimate heroes as role models, men and women we respected for their integrity, honesty and commitment to the betterment of this nation. Instead, I must agree with Ralph Waldo Emerson who stated that *"Imitation is suicide"*...a form of psychic suicide via the death of our spiritual uniqueness. Finally, to really nail it down—we hear from the great

English poet Samuel Johnson: "No (wo)man ever yet became great by imitation". Thus we see that imitation is another way of saying *"I can't do better!"*

If you stop thinking about yourself and realize there are people out there who always need help...do what you can for them and you'll be doing for yourself as well. Harvey Firestone once said that "You get the best out of others when you give the best of yourself!" Very true, but let's not forget that when we give the best of ourselves we also *become* the best, and isn't that what life is really about? Do unto others before they do unto you is great advice, *if* you only do good unto others.

# One Hundred Thirty Nine _____

# Love and Positive Living

It looks as though the connection is finally being made, between love and positive living. And why not, when the daily news seem to get worse each time you buy a newspaper or turn on your TV. Bad news brings anger to people, and anger turns into frustration. Frustration becomes hatred. Since we cannot for the most part attack directly that which angers us we *sublimate* our rage. This means that eventually the people nearest to us get the brunt of our ill feelings The ones closest to us are generally family..the ones we profess to love. And thus my subject matter for now. Love!

I'm not referring to the physical love we are so carelessly exposed to these days through the media, the movie houses and television. I'm speaking about the type of love the old songs *sing* about, the old poems *praise*, and the old paintings by the masters *portray* so elegantly. I'm also not alluding to the type of sterile love so poorly described in my *"fictionary"*: "a strong affection or attachment to someone" What an outrageous definition for the most important word in the English language!

Any psychologist can tell you that it is impossible to love anyone unless you first love yourself. After all, you cannot give away something you don't have. I don't mean the "gee, I'm cute an and lovable" type of personal infatuation. I mean a true *feeling good* about oneself. I refer to a self-love built on the qualities of honesty, integrity, kindness and genuine interest for others. Also, self-forgiveness for being human and thus prone to human errors, based on erroneous people judgements. My definition includes self-respect and humanitarianism, wherein we are motivated to help those unable to help themselves.

Dr. Karl Menninger, preeminent psychiatrist and founder of the world-class Menninger Clinic in Topeka, Kansas explained love this way: "Love *cures* people. Both the ones who give it and the ones who receive it!" What an easy, cost-free way to eliminate all sorts of psychosomatically self-induced illnesses. If it's true that we punish ourselves for "sins" by becoming sick it stands to reason that we can also help to heal ourselves by removing the original cause (i.e. guilt). Otherwise we're programming as bleak a future as our past.

Perhaps we should pay more attention to the bumper sticker I saw recently which read: "God loves you whether you like it or not!" This is known as unconditional love...the kind parents are supposed to have for their children, but many don't!

Love is a gift from our Creator, handed down to us at birth. True love begins from within. Look for it inside your head and heart. If it feels right, it's good for you! *Live it!*

# EPILOGUE

Over a half-century ago, Napoleon Hill wrote in his new classic work, THINK AND GROW RICH: "Whatever the mind of man can *conceive* and *believe*, man can *achieve*"..I'd like to rephrase that quote for you and print it below. Read it three times, right now.

Whatever *my* mind can conceive and believe, I can achieve!

Whatever *my* mind can conceive and believe, I can achieve!

Whatever *my* mind can conceive and believe, I can achieve!

You're still a bit skeptical, aren't you? You're sitting there judging and thinking..."I've heard all this stuff about Positive Thinking before, and it doesn't work!"

You know what? I agree with you. Positive thinking by itself doesn't work. You can sit around thinking positive thoughts all day long and nothing will change. To gain permanent control of your life, you have to transform the philosophy of positive thinking into the *reality* of positive *living*! You must put those positive ideas into active use in your life.

I shared many ideas with you in this book on *How To* do it.

This is *Not* a self-improvement book...it is a *Self-Discovery* book! I truly believe we are all born with an inner spring of strength, which can propel us to whatever destination we wish to reach. If you are not satisfied (enthusiastic would be a much better word) with your life right now...if you are not accomplishing all you once believed you could, it is because this inner strength has been covered up by thousands of layers of dust and dirt. The ideas discussed at length in this book will wash away the now outdated mental dust 'n dirt, and allow you to live your dreams. Remember that God's greatest creation in the universe was born to *win*...and it is our duty to do so! Here are some end-result examples of what you can become when you begin to use the concepts outlined in the preceding chapters:

—You will win respect and appreciation from your friends, family and business associates.

—You will feel truly good about yourself for the first time in your life, permanently.

—You will communicate your ideas effectively to other people.

—You will be able to motivate your family, co-workers and subordinates to get their work done more quickly and efficiently.

—You will discover why conventional goal-setting does not work.

—You will learn to target your activities to get what you want out of life.

—You will be able to help the people you care most about to get what they want out of life.

—You will begin to look forward with enthusiasm to each and every new day.

—You will eliminate the major causes of stress in your life.

—You will be much healthier than ever before.

Are you still unconvinced? Does it sound to you as though I am promising an awful lot...all for the purchase of this book? I'm really not, when you consider that we were all born with the instinct, intuition, insight, inspiration and imagination needed to dream of the stars, and the abilities to reach them.

In other words, the powers to accomplish all you dream of already belongs to you! You just need to *uncover them*, and learn to use them habitually.

Somewhere deep inside you there is a small voice telling you that you don't have to settle for your present life...that you *deserve more*! (If that voice was not there, neither would you be here, reading this book right now.)

That same small voice is probably asking you about my right to write this book...i.e., my credentials for a book on Positive Living. Well, the truth of the matter is, I am an S.O.B. on life. That is, a Solution-Oriented-Being. I am not P.O.d...Problem-Oriented, as most of us are.

I am now solution-oriented because I've been there...knee-deep in my own problems, and unable to move, paralyzed. Didn't like it one bit. With my minority background, refugee experiences and religious intolerance, I have known real, deep down and dirty pain. My childhood little friends were anger, hatred, frustration, despair and much, much fear. I grew up with what I now call a Superior Inferiority Complex. (Superior because my inferiority was greater than any one I knew.)

I tried several disciplines in psychology for help; what I discovered was that the best hand for help was attached to my wrist. I thus began a journey into introspection, a quest for knowledge of the self. It is still on-going at this writing. I read books, books, books; I attended movies and lectures...all about great men and women who *overcame* their past selves.

Former obstacles became hurdles...to be jumped over! I became a very good salesman; I was able to lose 38 pounds, which never found a home on me again. And most important, I was able to make my final marriage work.

As a professional speaker, I find that disrobing mentally in front of my audiences builds trust, an absolute *must* if they are to buy my message. By disrobing mentally, I mean letting my persona out...i.e., the *real me*! The one I can finally love, and approve of. I know that if I can do it, you can.

I have shown it can be done.

I'm doing it *now*!

You can, too!